TRULY SILLY

TRULY
SILLY

NICK RYAN

Troubador Publishing Ltd
Unit E2 Airfield Business Park,
Harrison Road, Market Harborough,
Leicestershire. LE16 7UL
Tel: 0116 2792299
Email: books@troubador.co.uk
Web: www.troubador.co.uk

ISBN 978 1836280 187

British Library Cataloguing in Publication Data.
A catalogue record for this book is available from the British Library.

Printed and bound by CPI Group (UK) Ltd, Croydon, CR0 4YY
Typeset in 11pt Minion Pro by Troubador Publishing Ltd, Leicester, UK

This book is dedicated to everyone who has contributed to its silliness, both knowingly and unknowingly.

FOREWORD 1

Unlike most authors, Dad didn't care for books. I only ever saw him physically reading one in my entire life (Clint Eastwood's biography during a long layover at Athens airport), and heard tell of him reading a second, over twenty years later (Bob Mortimer's autobiography at home in Derrynacoulagh).

Dad cared a lot more about funny stories. Specifically, telling funny stories. He was good at it too, very good, a natural born spellbinder. So that's how I like to think of this book; Dad sitting down and regaling you with a few of his favourites, laughing along with you - likely *more* than you - as he goes.

Many of you reading this will have heard these tales before. Many of that same many will have heard them more than once, no doubt with questionable consistency of detail (curiously, Dad would obsessively level this same charge of anecdotal exaggeration at his good friend and comedic rival Peter Yates-Round, a concerning projection likely reflected in the working title of this book: 'Funnier Than You').

A few of these choice cuts border on the insulting of course, but I'm certain no true harm was intended. Dad didn't work like that; everything and everyone was fair game. His mick-taking was a gesture of affection. The harder you were getting it, the more he liked you. Probably. Just in case, names have been altered to protect the innocent (though not quite enough to acquit the guilty).

All of which is to say, I can't tell you in good faith that this volume represents the definitive version of the recounted events… but having read through them, I'm certain it represents the definitive version of the author.

Witty, charming, generous, irreverent, slightly odd and mildly (to middlingly) offensive, with a final page turned far too soon.

These stories are truly silly. They are also truly Dad.

With a little imagination, you can even hear his voice again.

Patrick Ryan

FOREWORD 2

Rick Bryan you say? … No, never heard of him.

I knew a Nick Ryan once though, knew him well, a grand fella he was. Very good at the old music, you know, and funny with it. He could find humour in a pile of old stones, have you laughing before you could say "I`ll have a large box of suppositories please". Never laughed like I did when in his company, egged each other on I suppose. Split your sides laughing you could, fit to burst and tears running down your face … ah such times we had.

I remember the tale of The Sizzler, some kind of jape that was but if you want to know more then of course you`ll have to read the book. You won`t be disappointed I can tell you.

Oh yes… he was a grand fella and a dear friend - I miss him every day.

Robin Slater

CONTENTS

1

REDLIGHTITUS

I start this collection of anecdotes with a story that was related to me by a wonderful singer with whom I used to work during the eighties. His name was Nick Curtis (RIP) and he was present as the following events unfolded.

As a preface to this story I should explain that musicians in general - and brass players in particular - are wags. They're blessed with a keen sense of humour which they're ever ready to flaunt. The 'safety in numbers' principle probably applies here, boosting the musicians' confidence to react with rib-tickling ripostes at every toot when they're hired as a section, which brass players often are.

My friend Nick Curtis was booked one day to attend a recording session at a studio complex in Wembley. He was told by the fixer that he would be one of ten singers in a chorale.

It sounded like a big deal and sure enough, when Nick arrived at the studio, he discovered that most of London's top session musicians and singers had been assembled to perform on this major recording project.

The creative team's objective was to record the entire music score for a big blockbuster film which was in production at the time, and they'd secured the largest studio at London's CTS Studios complex in which to do it.

The musical line-up comprised a rhythm section with extra percussion, piano, keyboards, strings, woodwind, brass, singers and a harp; a total of perhaps eighty musicians, all under the direction of the music producer, the conductor and the composer. A few film company executives too were up in the studio's control room – loafing around and 'checking on progress' the way the suits normally do.

When the members of the orchestra were finally set up and in position ready to record, the producer called for quiet and they ran through the first 'cue' (the technical term for a section of film music).

Oh-oh. An added complication was that the music had been composed to synchronise with the on-screen action and therefore it had to be recorded with reference to the images. The conductor was responsible for guiding the tempo so that the sound synchronised with the picture, exactly as the composer had intended.

The first cue was distinguished by a short harp solo, about thirty seconds or so from the beginning of the piece. After they'd rehearsed that section a couple of times, the orchestra played the entire cue to iron out any other musical issues. Next, the conductor asked for a run-through with picture, so that the synchronisation points could be checked.

Everything went well – the conductor, composer and producer were happy. Just a few aspects were discussed and then finally, they were ready to record the first piece; the film's intro theme.

This fact was announced by the producer up in the control room, high above the studio floor.

"OK quiet please everyone. Project Amadeus. Cue One. Take One."

Right after the words 'Take One', the studio engineer activated a bright red light, which was a warning to everyone in the vicinity that recording was currently taking place so people should keep schtum.

Once the recording light was glowing, the conductor's voice led the orchestra with a count-in.

And they were off! Big sound.

Things went swimmingly for thirty seconds or so... but then, calamity!!

The harpist made a ghastly fist of his little solo bit. It rather sounded as if he'd selected a pair of leather gardening gauntlets for his big moment. If so, it was certainly not the wisest of choices for a man in charge of forty seven strings!

The producer's voice suddenly boomed out from loudspeakers somewhere on high as the orchestra ground to a halt.

"Hold it. Hold it! Stop! Harp mistake! Back to the top please. Wait for the picture... OK. Cue One. Take TWO."

Surely our harpist wasn't the same musician that had just played his part so perfectly in rehearsal.

With the red light still on, the orchestra immediately recommenced. Sadly though after thirty seconds or so, the clanger was repeated.

"No! Stop!!"

What's going on? That hand-fisted harp bit was at risk of becoming an established feature of the film's action-packed title sequence!

Not if the producer had anything to do with it though.

"Top again please everyone."

So, with ashen executive faces peering down through the control room window, everyone went back to the 'top' (muso-speak for 'the beginning')… for a third time.

"Cue One. Take Three."

And due to another repeat of the musical mishap…

"Cue One. Take *FOUR!*"

"Sorry."

A fourth disastrous attempt! Albeit this time with the word 'Sorry!' appended.

But 'sorry' just wasn't good enough. Time wasted in the studio is money wasted… big money as it happens, and by Take Four, this fact was being communicated in no uncertain terms to Louie the Hapless Harpist. A small deputation had gathered around him at this stage, including the composer, the producer, the conductor and the recording engineer. Voices were raised in exasperation as the production team demanded perfection.

It was finally agreed that Louie would spend some time practising the offending harp solo bit over and over and over, until it was so familiar, that the cock-up could never again be repeated.

Never *EVER*.

The embarrassed harpist obediently followed orders and set about his atonement – boring everyone senseless as he did so. Meanwhile, the production company executives nervously consulted their watches… and their calculators.

Eventually, the now familiar voice from above boomed once more.

"Right, Ladies and Gentlemen. Thank you for your patience there. Back to your places please. We'll try again. OK, Louie?"

Louie nodded convincingly. He was ready this time. Brimming with confidence. The intense rehearsal period seemed to have really paid dividends. He even managed to squeeze in a couple of extra renditions just before the count-in! A bid to salvage his visibly crumbling reputation, no doubt… and it did do that to be fair - his execution was, by now, reliably note perfect.

Great stuff! A recharged atmosphere of relief and elan instantly permeated the entire studio.

"OK, everybody! Stand by. This is the one! Take Five!"

The producer's crass optimism lasted… well, as you've probably guessed, approximately thirty seconds – 'til the harp bit of course.

"STOP! No No *NO* LOUIE!!! *HOLD IT!* And again straight back to the top please everyone! Picture! Go GO *GO!!*"

The producer could barely contain his anger – especially when he realised that his subsequent announcement would likely contain the two words 'Take' and 'Six'.

"Take Six!!"

Thought so. The pressure was on and so was the red light… as it had been for the bones of half an hour!

Poor Louie. The tension was palpable as the orchestra lumbered towards his big moment for this, the sixth time. Here it comes! The introductory bars, the piano bit, the woodwind… Everyone was willing him to please, *PLEASE* get it right. Surely this time he'd crack it! The session was falling way behind schedule and it was all Louie's fault! He *had* to get it right despite the pressure. Overtime fees alone for eighty musicians would be prohibitive.

Mind you, Take Six was sounding great so far – as if it *was* going to be The One. Yes, they're approaching the 27th second, the 28th, 29th… and here it comes! 30! And Yesssss! HE'S *DONE I…*

Oh No! Another dud!

'Poi-oi-oi-oi-oing'

And a broken string! Tension has a lot to answer for.

The producer's manic screams indicated that a Take Seven was probably on the cards.

"*LOUIE! NO! NO!!* Stop, please. Everyone *just STOP!!*"

The orchestra eventually ground to a frustrated halt again, leaving a desolate, hushed silence of disbelief hanging there in that vast room.

Oh, Louie.

Suddenly the sonic void was purged by a distant, loutish bellow. It came from a source somewhere deep in the bowels of the brass section.

"OH *FER FFFUCK'S SAKE! GIVE IT 'ERE!*"

There was a shocked hush across the room and then… a thunderous explosion of uncontrollable, raucous laughter from the entire orchestra! (Even Louie saw the funny side – although the best he could muster was a soppy grin.)

The racket must have continued for two minutes or so, as the massed musicians all reacted to the trumpeter's absurd offer. Then spontaneous applause broke out! It was so loud that it threatened to drown out the producer's rampant voice.

"Take Seven please, ladies and gentlemen. TAKE. SEVEN. *PLEASE!*"

What a hero of a harpist! All the angst and pressure that had been building up since Louie first plucked nearly an hour earlier was now dissipated and the musicians were relaxed and ready to go again.

As a result, Take Seven was absolutely perfect. A corker apparently.

Next!

Trouble is, once that red light goes on, the old stress levels do tend to shoot up a bit... don't they, Louie?

2

A COLLATING PROBLEM

The lifeblood of every successful advertising agency is new business. Its staff is constantly engaged in the pursuit of additional advertisers to expand the agency client-list and thereby maximise its income.

The bigger the brand, the bigger the advertising budget and the bigger the budget, the bigger the agency income.

So the stakes can be pretty high.

In the late seventies, Lintas, the advertising agency for which I once worked, was fortunate enough to be invited to pitch competitively for not one but *two* big-spending clients. One was Bowater Scott – a pulp and paper company specialising in packaging and absorbent tissue type products and the other was Rowntree's, the long-established confectionery company.

The only problem was that both these new business pitches were timed to run concurrently with in-house presentations due to be made at Lintas HQ on consecutive days.

Creative teams, media executives, client liaison and particularly secretarial services were all under great pressure as the pitch deadlines neared, but finally, after weeks of work, the presentations were over and done with.

It was out of our hands now. We could do no more.

There was a certain atmosphere of relief, suppressed elation and quiet confidence back in our offices as we awaited confirmation of the anticipated glad tidings.

All the agency's ideas had been well-received and the executives from both of the potential client companies had by now retreated to consider the presentation documents detailing our agency's specific marketing and media proposals.

All we had to do at Lintas was simply sit back and wait for news of the final decisions.

It was all looking very promising. Favourable rumours around town were leading us to believe that we might even have won *both* of the pitches!

Of course, that was before we noticed the heading on page 12 of the Rowntree's presentation document.

It read:-

POST-COITAL DRIP

Yeah... Shame, after all that work.

3

SHOW BUZZYNESS

Mark was not his real name and singing was not his real game, but Jeff Shark was nominally the lead singer of the first group I was ever in.

We were a 'beat group' called Mark and the Tempters and I was introduced to the idea of band membership by my friend Don Rickman who was the Tempter on guitar. He kindly explained to the other members that I was interested in joining the band and more to the point, had eighteen quid to prove it.

Fiscal solvency seemed to be the sole prerequisite of full band membership.

Hence, it wasn't very long before I was being introduced to my new bandmates, Tim, Jeff and Ron.

On drums was Tempter Tim Spantury. Now Tim had a unique approach to drum-set hitting which saw him studiously avoid any contact whatsoever with the bass drum. In Tim's mind it was just one drum too many – a complication he could well do without. In fact, we were only aware that Tim's biggest drum had sonic potential when he clumsily tripped over the spring-loaded pedal one day and, for the first time ever, activated the beater. On impact the huge drum issued an almighty foundation-rocking BOOM.

I remember Tim looked as shocked as the rest of us when it went off!

Yes it's fair to say that Tempter Tim utilised his bass drum as merely a kind of 'rock modesty-board' – a handy place for the band's name and logo.

The Tempter on piano, Ron Vantry, was the musical director of the band and the only member with discernible talent. It was Ron who encouraged me to invest my eighteen smackers in a crude, homemade bass guitar. This was my passport, of course, to becoming a fully legit Tempter.

And sure enough, in no time at all I was to be found up there on stage, tempting real, live audience members!

Mark, aka Jeff (he answered to both names) was the owner of a shiny new Reslo ribbon microphone at that time, which was '*de rigueur*' in the heady days of the beat boom. It was a foolish purchase on Jeff's part however, as it tended to faithfully reproduce every nuance of Mark aka Jeff's vocal impotence.

Audiences were suddenly aware that he was shite and, thanks to his new-fangled purchase, 'loud and clear' shite.

Luckily for me though, the loudness and shite-yness of Mark's contribution to The Tempters' unique sound was not lost on the other members of the group. Since his spotless new Reslo was sensitive on both sides, there was a vacant position available on the 'other side' of Mark's mic. Consequently, I was encouraged by Ron, Don and Tim, to claim this spot and bolster our lead singer's performance as best I could.

Maybe one day I'd blossom into a kind of Mark - a 'Mark 2' as I imagined it - as if wrestling with a hefty homemade bass guitar wasn't enough of a challenge!

My first ever 'on-stage' vocal was apparent in our cover of a song called 'Farmer John' by 'Hep Stars' during which my sole vocal contribution was to mumble the phrase 'A-looka-here!' Not exactly singing of course but a vocal contribution nonetheless. On stage I used to get quite nervous as that three-word utterance loomed large on my horizon, prompting me to begin the traipse over to Mark aka Jeff who'd then begrudgingly offer me the arse end of his new Reslo. Why he couldn't schlep over to me occasionally or compromise with a rendezvous somewhere central, like in front of the ever-dormant bass drum, I never discovered.

Another thing that irked me was my certainty that Mark always whipped the mic away from my mouth needlessly early – well before I'd finished performing my line. It wasn't a conspiracy theory - it was my mother who first noticed this nasty trait of Mark's. And she was right. I think she had a word with Ron on my behalf.

Listen.

'A-look-ah...'

That's all I could ever hear of my special augmentation and I assure you I gave it absolutely everything I had.

Hey! Where's my 'a-here'!?

Our front man was as silent as our bass drum.

Of course I can't claim to have *transformed* this particular song with my brief vocal contribution but it did at least offer the audience a two-and-a-half second respite from Mark aka Jeff's drone.

More importantly, I was now considered 'a bit of a vocalist'.

Mark Shark, on the other hand, was a dead man singing.

A personnel change was surely in the offing for Mark and the boys. Well, for the boys anyway.

Doubtless 'the Tempters' without a 'Mark aka Jeff' was unthinkable, so once we'd jettisoned Jeff (nice alliteration there Jeff don't you think?), poached another vocalist called Len Dodd and changed our name to Soundsa Round (yes, that was the spelling), we were all set to conquer the world.

But there was much to do.

While a new repertoire was being hastily prepared by Ron, Len and Tim, Don and I got working on the electronic side of things.

Competition between the local semi-professional groups at that time was fierce, and with the phrase 'got working on the electronic side of things' I'm alluding to a devilish device invented by our own Don Rickman.

I'd like to stress, however, that what follows was in no way 'band policy'.

Don was the Tempters' technical and electronics wizard (every semi-pro band has one) and somehow he managed to construct a very special gadget, the sole function of which was to emit an irritatingly loud buzzing noise when in the vicinity of band amplification. Don and I called this invention 'The Sizzler'. It was just what the doctor ordered to give us an edge over our rivals.

We were going to blow all our competitors right out of the water with this thing! Not by dint of constant practising. No. Not by the relentless study of advanced musical theory.

No. Not by chromatic chordal and melodic progressions. No. And not - certainly not - by plain, simple, hard graft.

No. We would achieve it, merely by the annihilation of our rivals' sound! Simple.

The Sizzler was first employed during a church hall dance at Leigh-on-Sea, where Southend's most prestigious beat group was due to top the bill at a well-publicised event.

(The band shall remain nameless because some of them were big lads with tattoos and, as I recall, fiery tempers.)

A sizeable crowd was guaranteed at this, the band's first ever appearance at Saint Margaret's church hall. As luck would have it, we learned during bench-testing of the Sizzler that the band's lead guitarist, Chris, suffered from a distressing aversion to the sight of blood and/or guts. It was apparently important that he be protected from exposure to such viscera.

Hmmmm.

This was a very appealing bonus in our opinion, which unfortunately we were unable to resist. In fact I, who had a Saturday job at a local butcher's shop, was immediately charged with the task of procuring a grisly bull's eye (or two), especially for use at the upcoming church hall dance. It was 'belt and braces' really – if the Sizzler's tiresome buzz didn't sabotage the gig, a bloodshot bull's eye complete with severed optic nerve surely would.

So, the big night arrived. Don and I strolled into the hall, our pockets bulging with electrical components, spare batteries and bovine body parts. We headed over to greet the band while they were setting up and wished them all a good gig.

Meanwhile, the hall was filling up quite nicely. The parish of Saint Margaret of Antioch was going to be the very first community in Christendom to experience the Sizzler in action.

And soon enough… Yes, it's showtime!

"Good evening, ladies and gentlemen, please put your hands together for 'The Nameless Big Fellas'!!!"

To rapturous applause, the band burst into life. Christ, they're good! I noticed Don eagerly rummaging in his jacket pocket.

"Whoa, Don! Relax. There's no rush".

I fingered the glutinous contents of my own pocket. It was oozing bullish fluids and was consequently quite whiffy.

Nice.

Everything was going precisely to plan.

We decided to give it half an hour or so before debuting our invention, because people were still coming in. We felt that it was vital that we coordinate our electronic spoiler with the bull's eye effect, to produce a double-whammy sabotage from which there'd be no return.

At about 8:55 p.m., Don gave me a wink and discreetly fired up the Sizzler.

Drrrrrrrrrrrrrrrrrrrrrrrrrrrr!

It was quieter than we'd anticipated but it sat there sweetly in the mix, hinting at havoc. Don and I exchanged knowing smiles as we clocked furtive glances of concern darting between the musicians up on the stage.

Looks like they're losing it.

How rewarding.

When I think of all the hours Don spent crouched over the workbench with that faithful soldering-iron of his… Without him, where would we be now?

It wasn't too long before puzzled dancers began leaving

the floor in droves with accusatory glances over towards the stage area from where the band's interference was issuing.

Oh and raised voices too! Sounds like the band's notoriously fiery tempers were starting to fray.

Reluctantly, they soldiered on, but one by one they each tapped out. Right out. They were no match for the Sizzler.

Don reached into his pocket and after a few creative flourishes - onoff-off-on-offonoff - there was silence.

Everyone breathed a sigh of relief. That tiresome sizzle had been so aggravating. At last it had ceased though, thank God. The fault, whatever it was, seemed to have rectified itself just as the inevitable announcement was being made.

"Sorry about this, ladies and gentlemen. Err, as you heard there, we've got a slight technical problem I'm afraid… a bit of a hum. So, we'll take a short break and be back with you in fifteen minutes or so. We'll try to sort it out. Sorry about that. Thank you. See you later."

Next on the agenda for us was a backstage visit to feign sympathy and see what we could do to help the wretched musicians. By this time they were desperately tugging leads, examining connections and arguing loudly amongst themselves, even though the buzz had finally abated. Well, not exactly abated. Don couldn't resist a cheeky, final blast during the silence of the enforced hiatus. It was 'for good measure', he told me later.

The obligatory pause and ensuing mayhem of course provided the perfect conditions for us to initiate phase two of our dastardly plot… deployment of the 'mince pie'. (Estuary rhyming slang for 'eye')

While the band members were deeply distracted by their electronic woes, Don and I carefully positioned our rancid, optical organ centre stage, in the shadows, close to the lead guitarist's foot pedal. It'd be staring up at him once he returned to his playing position.

With the Sizzler dormant in Don's pocket, 'The Nameless Big Fellas' were soon re-mounting the stage and gingerly plugging instruments back into their volatile amplification system. Worryingly, the cause of the interference had not been identified by the band and Don and I were concerned that the problem could rear its ugly head again at any moment. In fact, we were sure it would.

Overall though, the vibe coming from the bandstand was one of renewed vigour and enthusiasm. Good to see.

But would it last?

Don and I didn't think so.

The band looked 'ready to rock'... but we were anticipating a dramatically truncated set, especially if that lead-guitarist chap casually squinted into the darkness down near his pedal.

As the five lads prepared to boogie, the drummer kept the audience fully updated - against a limp and inappropriate Latin-y, bossa-nova type rhythm he'd created especially for nights such as this...

'Tic-ticca-tic-tic-tiddle ica-tic-ticca-icca-etcetera'

"Ladies and gentlemen, sorry about the interruption to our show tonight. We had a few gremlins there for a while but we've sorted it all out and now we're back to entertain you."

Sparse applause from a rapidly diminishing and disenchanted audience was the only discernible reaction from the NBF fans.

'Tic-ticca-tic-tic-tiddle ica-tic-ticca-icca-etcetera'

Here he goes again.

'Tic-ticca-tic-tic-tiddle ica-tic-ticca-icca-etcetera'

"...So we'd like to start the second half with an instrumental number featuring our lead-guitarist, Chris. It's a tune by 'The Chantays' and it's called 'Pipeline'. We hope you like it."

Oh, how gratifying. An instrumental! The delicate lead guitarist's party-piece! And he was reckoned to be one of the best guitarists in the whole Leigh-on-Sea area. Wonder how he'll cope with a bit of pressure?

"Lights!" We'll soon find out. Here we go.

"A-one-two-three-four!" The band burst into life and started cooking. (You could even smell sausages!)

Unfortunately, from our position in the hall we couldn't quite see the boys on stage, but it was in fact much funnier to savour the audio component alone, especially as things began to deteriorate.

I'd say the doomed musician up there first noticed our 'gift' about a minute or so into the number. That was when the first subtle signs of disorientation seemed to cloud his performance. Yup, he's seen it. Don and I nodded at each other. He's definitely seen it.

An ear-piercing, discordant *'pweeeeeeeeeeeeeE'* confirmed our suspicions.

Slowly but surely, Chris's interpretation of this tune began to turn 'unique' before our very ears, as the notes of the melody took a surreal twist. His articulation had completely gone to pot.

We moved away quickly to find a better vantage point from where our victim could be fully observed. At first we couldn't locate him at all, but he was eventually unveiled in the shadows over at the back of the stage. Pale and wan, he cut a miserable figure, slumped there against his amplifier. He was in a trance, staring vacantly at the floor.

Chris was a fighter though – credit where it's due. Occasionally, a tortured 'doioioiiiing' could be heard feebly twinging from his amp but, unfortunately, nothing remotely resembling 'Pipeline'. Pity really – it was one of my favourites. A group dad mounted the stage and kindly tried to stand Chris back up on his feet again, but it was pointless. Shouting loudly into the man's ear served no useful purpose either. He was in a daze and transfixed by something down there at his feet.

Certainly the thumb and forefinger of Chris's right hand still clutched an orange pick and periodically twitched a bit, but as for 'Pipeline', it was plainly not a viable proposition.

Chris, I'm afraid – trooper that he was - was done for.

Send us another lead-guitarist please. This one's broken!!

Against all odds, Don and I were forced to acknowledge the professionalism that the 'the Big Fellas' exhibited that night. They gamely tried to keep the show on the road as if nothing was wrong but it was a futile exercise.

You see, Don had cruelly re-activated the Sizzler to maximise the on-stage mayhem. I must admit it was a laudable initiative on Don's part. The band didn't really stand a chance. They slowly ground to a halt as their ailing front man was gently escorted from the bandstand with a group dad supporting him on each side. His girlfriend followed loyally behind, carrying his Fender axe, which was by now soiled by some specks of vomit near the bridge pick-up.

"Testimony to his ordeal," Don observed.

What a sad spectacle they presented, slowly processing through the near deserted church hall.

Anyway, the last we saw of Chris he was dry retching in the recovery position out near the group's van. He'd been laid there by the paramedics. Fair play though, he never lost consciousness… not as far as we could tell.

"He just needs a bit of air! He'll be fine! Stand back! Give 'im some air!"

Any musicians out there interested in acquiring a Sizzler of their own should contact Don Rickman at Rickman Electronics, Rickman House, Duggyloss, Cyprus.

I've been asked to point out that Mark Shark claims he was *not* shite.

Drrrrrrrrrrrrr

SHOW BUZZYNESS

4

SQUARING DOWN

It was the qualifications that proved a stumbling block for me… a 'Grade E pass' in chemistry, physics and biology. It doesn't sound like an unattainable goal but actually it was… twice. Guy's Dental Hospital did its best to accommodate my apparent zeal for a career in dentistry by offering me a coveted place in their ranks. Sadly though, despite a punishing repeat year back at Westcliff High School for Boys, it was not to be.

I was totally incapable of pulling off three Grade E passes. Message received.

There was no hope whatsoever therefore, of my ever becoming a dentist.

After all, I just needed to consider the facts. I was an arty type. I had minimal interest in galvanometers, rabbit dissection, Bunsen burners and light refraction – that sort of stuff – so after a few seconds' reflection; I came up with a plan. The wisest choice would be to do absolutely nothing. It had served me so well in the past, I knew I couldn't go wrong. So that's it… I'd just tough it out for as long as necessary.

Yup, the decision was good as made. Stick with my holiday job as a dustman in the short term and wait 'til the perfect career, in combination with gravitational pull, fell into my lap.

This eventually did happen, in the form of an advert which captured my attention when it appeared in the Evening News one day – well, one evening actually. It was seeking to recruit a 'TV time buyer' for a vacancy at a London advertising agency. I'd never heard of this particular occupation but in my mind, the seductive letters T and V implied an exotic career somewhere in or on the periphery of show business.

Perfect.

Inaccurate.

With a celebrity-studded future in mind, I attended an interview and was soon offered a plum job at that big, swanky advertising agency up in London.

Lights, camera, action!

Me, a TV executive! Can't wait to meet all the stars.

Madison Avenue here I come! Well… actually, it was Lansdowne Avenue at that early stage of my career, then down Beach Avenue to Chalkwell Station, Fenchurch Street, Tower Hill to Blackfriars tube and finally a brisk walk round the corner to New Fetter Lane and Lintas.

Once I'd received official confirmation of my successful bid for a career in TV, I submitted a full and formal notice of my intentions by contacting all interested parties 'on the dust' at Rochford.

Most of my colleagues wished me well when they heard the news. The foreman at the depot, however, tried his best to reroute my career path.

"Leaving, Nick? Well… it's up to you of course my friend, but if you're interested, I could have you *driving* in a couple of months!"

It was obvious that the top brass on the council saw me as a future luminary of waste management, probably because I signed my name with proper joined-up writing when we were handed our wages every Friday. Most of my workmates went for a shaky X to confirm receipt of their earnings.

So certainly I was destined for great things had I remained at Rochford Council, no doubt about that. On the down side however, during the first five months of working for the Council, I hadn't met one single celebrity. There just seemed to be a dearth of them in the local Essex communes.

The Lintas opportunity on the other hand even featured TV as part of the job description! Plus! More money too! No contest. It was going to be the Ad Game for me.

So, tempting as the foreman's generous proposal had seemed, my heart was by now set on becoming a junior TV time buyer – maybe even a senior TV time buyer one day!

I politely turned down the enticing counter-offer, bade the lads on dustcart YNO 696 goodbye and soon found myself commuting daily to 'the big smoke.'

OK, so I must admit that I haven't met that many celebrities since I joined the ad game but they're probably all over the place up there in the metropolis. Just got to flush 'em out… it's all to do with confidence really isn't it? Inner confidence.

Unfortunately though, confidence wasn't really my strong suit. As junior TV time buyers go, quite frankly I was not really officer material. I was a timid and shy junior TV time buyer. Awkward in phone conversations, I wore my suit jacket at all times regardless of weather conditions and tried not to engage with women, or for that matter… men.

I persisted with this personal policy for at least the first three months of my advertising career, until one afternoon I encountered…

Rodney.

Like me, he was a junior TV buyer, but that's where the similarity ended. Rodney was assured, sporty, gregarious and good at his job. Oh, and he had a famously short temper as well.

In fact, he was 'ard as nails, people used to say. No one tangled with Rodney, that's for sure. Not if they had any sense.

I tangled with Rodney though. I tangled big time.

It was the day he burst into our office, charged over to my desk and in his Hoddesdon twang demanded;

"Can you play foo'ball?"

Now I'd never met this chap before but he didn't exactly ingratiate himself to me with his abrupt manner. He saw no need for an introduction, no exchange of pleasantries, just those four bare words. 'Can – you – play – foo'-ball?' He apparently had the task of rounding up an agency soccer team for a match the following Sunday.

Anyway, choosing to overlook his abrasive interruption, I decided on a polite but firm response.

"No."

I think he sussed that I wasn't best pleased with him but his reaction, his *over*-reaction was, in my humble opinion, 'well out of order' – as they probably say in 'oddesdon.

"You cunt."

What!!!!? I didn't really take it in at first. What did he just say to me? Just a second, matey! OI! Come back here!!!

He'd gone.

Rodney had presumably loped off in search of that full complement for Sunday's match.

I, meanwhile, sat there at my desk, fuming, stunned and instantly apoplectic with indignation and rage... Who is this ignorant bastard anyway?!... I'm not accepting that from anybody!

Suddenly I was on my feet and striding away in hot pursuit of the Lintas lout. Rodney and I had unfinished business. Where is he? Which way d'he go?

Ah! There he is! In the big open-plan office next door, still touting for a team I s'pose.

I barged in, marched over and tapped him sharply on the shoulder. I elected to roar my message for maximum impact.

"OI! CAN YOU PLAY THE ABYSSINIAN NOSE FLUTE?"

A pause of suspicion preceded Rodney's reply.

"...No."

"YOU *CUNT*!"

Absolute silence.

Typewriters, 'phones, distant traffic, conversations, everything froze, as I stood there with a sort of triumphant, yet inane grin on my face. I was particularly proud that my delivery of the colourful slur featured a strong attack on the first consonant – the 'K' sound. This was enhanced, I felt, by a slight narrowing of the eyes and baring of teeth. It's difficult to describe in the written word but I'm confident that aficionados of this particular smear would surely have applauded my execution.

Anyway, I digress. The important thing was, justice had been served. I served it and Rodney sucked it up. He then sidled off out of the office with his tail between his legs. That's how I saw it anyway. I was busy revelling in his public humiliation… what a triumph!

By this stage, the room was thronged with intrigued co-workers summoned by the sound of loud cursing, raised voices and the promise of imminent violence.

My silly, smug countenance remained fixed in position throughout as I inwardly gloated at the lesson Rodney had just been force fed. Not bad for a 'new boy' eh?

In contrast with my own expression though, my office colleagues were by now registering shock, disbelief, panic, and deep fear on their faces. People were uneasy. There didn't seem to be a single trace of admiration for my plucky challenge.

Pity.

Eventually, somebody spoke. It was Denis from accounts.

"Bit harsh Nick, don't you think? Foolhardy too I fear. Why ever did you call Rodney that word?"

"Because, Denis, that word is exactly what he called me when I told him I don't play football."

"No! He didn't. He didn't!" they all protested.

"He said you can't! Not… you… 'you-know-what'!"

"Did he?"

In unison, "Yeeaahss!"

"Really??! But…"

I began to ponder the evidential facts. What if I *had* misheard Rodney? It's true that I was somewhat unfamiliar with the nuances of the Hoddesdon burr at that particular time, but… surely… and I was distracted too…by Rodney's off-handed reaction.

Slowly the true reality of the whole ugly incident was beginning to seep into my brain. I replayed events over and over, substituting words. What if this? What if that? Until, finally, I came to the inexorable conclusion.

Oh my God! What a disaster!!

I raced up the corridor in a frenzied search for the 'ard man. Where did he go? I needed to offer my heartfelt apologies pronto and thereby mitigate any savagery that Rod (note the now chummy abbreviation of my new buddy's name) might be planning!

Eventually I tracked him down to some distant office on the third floor and tip-toed in so as not to startle the man. I composed my features into a mask of contrition as I cautiously approached but I noticed that Rod tensed when I walked in. I saw him tightly clench both fists. Yes, *both* fists! He was plainly preparing himself for some bold action.

Uh-oh… he's gonna lash out. Time for a change of plan.

Erm…

The only option as far as I could see, was to hastily recompose my demeanour from 'near tearful apologetic' to 'dangerously threatening'. Not an easy transition to pull off by any means.

I decided I'd begin our imminent altercation with an 'accidental' shoulder brush – no words exchanged and no eye contact. That should be helpful.

But then… where does that get me?

Oh God.

I scanned the room for some sort of prop to help endorse my tough-guy transformation.

Got one. That'll do. It wasn't ideal but I went for it anyway; a stray pencil, recently sharpened.

With all eyes upon me, I slowly withdrew my weapon of choice from its scabbard – an otherwise empty jam jar on one of the desks.

As I revealed my HB 'spear' to the anxious audience, I muttered quietly to myself;

"Ah, there it is."

I then swaggered assuredly out of the room – running the gauntlet no doubt, of an indignant, thuggish, Hoddesdon glare.

I'd like to think that my ballsy body language sent a shiver or two up Rodney's spine that Wednesday afternoon. Should teach him a lesson.

Fortunately, it never did come to blows between the two of us but Rodney and I did give each other an especially wide berth from that day forward.

'Respect', as they say in rap circles.

5

MEN AND MOTORS

In 1986, the Citroen 2CV was described by motoring correspondent Leonard John Kensell Setright as 'the most intelligent application of minimalism ever to succeed as a car... and a vehicle of remorseless rationality'.

I wholeheartedly agree, LJK. The *Deux Chevaux* was so much more than 'an umbrella on wheels', as it was unkindly described by less enthusiastic reviewers.

As a young motorist, I was such a fan that I owned a succession of these cars. Red ones, green ones, some as big as your head.

Yes, a spin in a 2CV was like an eternal fairground ride. It made motoring fun and bouncy and French.

My very first *Deux Chevaux* though, was black and orange courtesy of a rather sloppy manual paint job applied by the previous owner, and it had a dipstick for the fuel tank, a dipstick for the oil level and, some would say, a dipstick at the wheel.

Also, the 2CV windscreen wipers had no independent motor. They were powered by rotation of the speedometer cable, so they wiped only when the car was in motion. Ingenious, yet mental!

Its quaint but inconvenient collection of features, plus other age-related mechanical problems, eventually led to my hankering after a more recent 2CV – a later model, with all the bells and whistles. First though, I'd have to shift the old orange and black yoke.

I decided to place an advertisement in the motoring section of the Southend Standard newspaper and, to make it distinctive, I thought I'd give my sales spiel a nice, distinctive, Gallic flavour. Y'know, French car, French language.

It made a lot of sense.

Sorry, I beg your pardon. It made no sense at *all* – not to Southend Standard readers anyway. Of this I am positive.

After much deliberation, the wording I finally approved read as follows:

'**Citroen 2CV** *pour* sale with customised paintwork. *A saisir!* 94,000 miles *sur le compteur. Le prix?* £80 *seulement!*'

To my mind, the clever thing about my creation was that it promoted the selling features of the car in the mother tongue, but at the same time conjured a nice French 'ambiance'. You could almost hear the sound of *les accordions Bal-musette* coming off the page as you read it. Well, *I* could anyway… Almost.

Good stuff. By Thursday, I was all agog and standing by for a barrage of enquiries. Yup. Thursday's the day all right! That car will be sold and off my hands by the weekend!

Trust me.

Oh dear what a pity… I received *aucune reponse.*

The phrase *aucune reponse* is French for 'no response. None. Not one response. Not any responses'.

The next week, following a very robust exchange of views between the members of my sales team (which comprised me, my mother, sister and girlfriend), there appeared in the same publication a revised ad for my car – this time entirely in English. I was somewhat disappointed by my advisors' lack of creativity, but they were united in the belief that an English language version was the only way to go. They explained that 'the man on the Clapham omnibus' (whoever he is) would get a second chance to notice my automotive giveaway – and now, thanks to my team, he could actually understand it!

I begged to disagree.

Oh please I beg of you… let me disagree! Pleeeeeease.

As far as I was concerned, 'the man on the Clapham omnibus' was completely irrelevant to my campaign – for two reasons.

Firstly, this man from South West London doesn't need a car if he already rides in and around the capital on an omnibus. Secondly, the Southend Standard isn't even available in Clapham, so how is this anonymous Londoner ever going to see my ad?

As you can tell, I used weak humour in conversations with my family to distract from my overwhelming embarrassment about the failed, Frenchy-type approach. I still remained very positive about the sale though. It was a hell of a good buy, that car.

OK, I'm 20 quid down at the moment after funding the foreign language campaign. But so what?

Oh yeah. Fair enough, it's going to be another 20 notes for the full English revamp. That still leaves me about another 40 sovs to play with though… D'you notice my vocabulary has gone all 'motor trade-ish' as I impart to you the details?

I must admit that as Thursday approached, I was becoming a little nervous about how my potential customers were going to react when my motor was unveiled and then re-unveiled for a second time just a week later. It didn't bode well for an easy sale, I feared. My margins were pretty tight with all the advertising expenses n' stuff.

In fact, I was beginning to lose some confidence. Maybe I'd never manage to shift that bloody car.

I needn't have feared though. Soon after publication of the Standard on Thursday, our phone was ringing off the hook! Actually, there was only the one call, but I did knock it off the hook in my eagerness to answer.

So an arrangement was made with the caller for him and his wife to view my Citroen the following Saturday morning. I think they thought it was a 'snip' at just eighty nicker!

People often say 'and eighty nicker was a lot of money in those days.' But it wasn't. It was just dirt cheap!

What do they say in classified car ads? "First to view will buy!" I was more concerned about the 'only one to view'!

Anyway a young 'free spirited' couple presented themselves on our doorstep that Saturday morning and soon they were kicking tyres, asking searching questions and demanding receipts to support my exaggerated maintenance and repair claims.

What did they expect for eighty pounds anyway? As I've already implied, it wasn't a lot of money in those days.

Next, of course, they demanded a damn test-drive! Well I had to say yes… otherwise it was going to look like I was hiding something wasn't it? Yes OK… Get in. GET IN!

They had me over a barrel! It was imperative that I close the sale. Otherwise I'd never be able to afford the newer 2CV. It could cost me a hundred and fifty pounds, and that *was* a lot of money in those days.

So off we went for a spin and, to my surprise, during the test-drive these deceivingly tough cookies suddenly asked if we could jaunt over to their house in Eastwood, 'cos they'd forgotten to bring any money with them. I couldn't believe it. No money? Saucy hippies! How could you set off to go and buy a car with no money on you?!

Well, that's what they'd done… so I *had* to take them. They had me by the short and curlies.

"Yes of course, we'll drive over to Eastwood."

They only needed 80 quid for God's sake! That wasn't a lot of money in those days!

It was a good omen though. If they were looking for money, it was probably because they wanted to give some of it to me! They were keen and bursting to buy and I knew it. They knew I knew it too! I'd soon be wiping the floor with 'em – once we got to the negotiation stage! I had expenses to recoup.

When we arrived at their home, which was a perfectly respectable and un-hippyish semi on a typical Essex housing estate, they invited me in for a cuppa.

Why not? Empathy with the client and all that. It's what selling is all about isn't it? It's in the bag anyway but… nice cup o' tea? Yes please.

So in we went.

To my surprise, they had not one stick of furniture to their name… whatever their name was.

However, what they did have was a pet mongoose! It was shooting around the place like a demon, pausing only to defecate on the polished lounge floor tiles and gnaw at our shoes. This bloody herpestidae had the freedom of the entire ground floor of their home, which as a result, was skiddily treacherous to human traffic.

We downed a quick cuppa (standing up and clutching the sink for traction) and then continued the test-drive back to my house. I was by now refreshed and ready for some gritty negotiation.

Unfortunately, I felt that my bargaining position had been seriously undermined by this time though, due to the fact that I did quite like this couple. I had, after all, spent most of the morning in their company.

Also, I felt a bit sorry for them because they couldn't afford furniture and their family pet was a manic mongoose with IBS. I was beginning to suffer mixed emotions about the whole car transaction, but still… I did covet that later model 2CV, so the sale had to go ahead. No question.

Luckily I was in the advantageous position of knowing that they definitely wanted to buy my car and there, burning a hole in their mutual pocket, they had the 80 pounds to do it (which wasn't a lot of money in those days).

So here I am in the driving seat, so to speak. Let the cut and thrust of hard negotiation commence! The phrase 'Like candy from a baby' came to my mind. Ha-ha! No laughter though. I went for a wry smile.

The young man was the first to speak.

"Tell you what. I'll give you sixty pounds for your car."

"Oh. Twenty quid less than the asking price, eh? That's a discount of 25 per cent."

"Well that's my offer. Sixty pounds, yeah? For your car."

"Certainly not my friend."

I was decisive and firm. My turn now. Stand by, hippies.

"Make it… forty!"

"*Forty?!* Oh great! Thank you *so* much."

Shake.

Done.

That went rather well I thought.

I looked at the maths after they'd gone and realised that this hadn't quite been the lucrative deal I'd envisaged. What with the £20 wasted on the foreign language campaign, the client knocking me down by £20 and my own knock down of a further £20, I was left with… yes £20. Those 2CVs are very good on petrol, so I'm not even going to include fuel for the test-drive, cost of the car wash, tax, valeting service, wear and tear and so-on. That's all negligible as far as I'm concerned.

Yes, I was very happy. The sale was complete.

And 40 notes was quite a lot of money in those days.

Anyway, I explained it all to my girlfriend, and after listening to the whole story, she questioned (I presume sarcastically) why I didn't throw in a continental holiday for two as well!

Women don't really understand the cut, thrust and intricacies of buying and selling in the motor trade, do they?

6

DIVERSIFICATION

Years ago, I noticed a hilarious brass sign on a blue door of a building somewhere in County Sligo, Ireland. It read as follows:

EUGENE MULLANEY

DENTAL SURGEON AND PUNCTURE REPAIRS

I like to imagine that one slack day in the surgery, it slowly dawned on this entrepreneurial tooth doctor that his elevators, probes, excavators and forceps could well be used to expand the old business a bit.

So tractor tyres, air beds, bicycle inner-tubes, li-los, football bladders… bring 'em on!

And be sure to drop them back for their six-monthly check-up won't you? Things are a bit quiet at the moment.

7

SOME OLD CASTLE

Bryan Flater, Peter Davron and I were on our way to compete in the annual Castlebar Song Contest held in County Mayo, Ireland. Our song had been written by Bryan and me and was selected as a finalist, to be performed by our chosen singer - Peter Davron.

Even though we were travelling in my puny Citroen 2CV, we were ahead of schedule on the journey to Castlebar and had time for a bit of sight-seeing along the way. We decided that the next sign we encountered indicating a tourist attraction, we would follow.

We soon came upon a placard promoting a castle, the name of which none of us can now recall. Anyway, we followed the arrows and after a convoluted tour of the locality, we finally arrived at the entrance to a big field, guarded by a geriatric custodian holding a handwritten sign.

There was no sign of a castle. Just the sign of an admission-fee sign.

We needed advice, and the only person who could possibly help us was the ancient castle-gatekeeper.

Peter went over to consult the old codger and spoke loudly.

"Hello. How're you doing? We're wondering if we might, er, visit the castle today. Is that possible?"

The codger smiled and nodded but made no comment.

"Er, is it... far away? The castle?"

"Wha'?"

Ah, now we're getting somewhere.

"IS THE CASTLE FAR AWAY?"

"Oid say 'bout a moile... bot wid legs as long as yours, you'll probaly do it in haff de distance."

The old fogey was now directing his gnarled forefinger towards the gate. Maybe he had strict instructions not to reveal the castle until customers had coughed up. Even so, we were slightly suspicious as we could see neither hide nor hair of any castle whatsoever.

Surely the old-timer hadn't mislaid it!

Mr Flater then stepped in to give our doddery dude one last opportunity to collect an admission fee for the grand tour.

"So is it worth visiting then? The castle?"

"Not at all! Idn't it jost a poile of aul' stones."

"Oh. Right."

"Thank you. 'Bye!"

"Good lock, lads."

Something told us your man was probably not on commission.

8

SOME OLD POPE

Continuing our journey to Castlebar for its famous song contest, we were travelling across Ireland in the midst of Pope John Paul ll's official visit there. We tuned in on the car radio (barely audible above the roar of my 2CV's 602 cc engine) and regularly monitored the pontiff's progress. Currently, he was heading to the west of Ireland where thousands of the faithful had gathered.

I can only assume that on this particular day, a capable radio commentator was not available to RTE for the Galway gig, so they hurriedly appointed a neighbour of the CEO's granny, to report on the Pope's arrival at Galway airport.

He did reasonably well... except for a major problem with an everyday article of winter clothing.

Here's roughly what we heard:

"And yes, there he is! The Pope has finally arrived in Galway! He's at the top of the aeroplane steps now and, oh yes - he's waving to the thousands who've braved the cold weather to welcome him here to the west. What a momentous day this is! And now he's… er, he's descending the steps and looks to be in fine form despite the appalling conditions. Yes, he's well away, wrapped up there in his fine, er warm… er… em… er… er… his warm, erm… er…

COAT!"

Eventually I s'pose, somebody must have prompted our commentator. It's just an outer garment that we all would tend to wear during cold weather – designed to keep the wearer warm… C-O-A-T, isn't it? A coat.

9

THE HEALING

To visit my grandmother at our local mental hospital was an onerous task. The communal ward there was crammed with seriously disturbed patients – some of them pacing in tight circles, some slumped in stained armchairs. There was a deafening hubbub of gibberish and of course, the ubiquitous smell of urine.

My mother's mother could make no sense of her surroundings at all – thank God. She'd gaze out of the window down at the hospital car park – convinced that she was surveying the spectacular Mountains of Mourne 'sweeping down to the sea' (to quote the famous Irish song).

She'd repeatedly ask the same faltering question.

"Who are you?"

She had, in fact, not articulated anything remotely rational for many years.

Mary Bride, such was her mental decline, seemed unrecognisable now as the woman who raised my sister and me – the woman who generously moved into our house following my father's fatal car crash in 1956, to help her daughter cope with widowhood.

Due to the close connection that we'd forged with our grandmother over the years, it was very depressing to see her incarcerated amid all the chaos of a mental hospital.

So that's what inspired me to come up with my Alzheimer's cure.

I remember taking my sceptical sister and mother through the key points of the innovative strategy I'd developed.

It was a very simple idea and they're always the best aren't they, even in the complex world of mental health.

The basic foundation of my dementia recovery programme hinged on over-reaction to balderdash. Any rubbish that Granny uttered was to be answered with 'HED' – Highly Exaggerated Discombobulation. That's simply 'puzzlement' in layman's terms.

A furrowed brow, an expression of aggressive contradiction, a raised eyebrow, a grimace… I would use all the tools available to me to heal our poor dementia-ridden matriarch.

I was convinced that my intense facial reactions would indicate to Granny when she was talking bollocks.

She'd notice its effect on me and seek to correct her jumbled thought processes.

Moreover… I was confident that, given time, she'd re-learn how to use her powers of reason. The family scoffed at my naivety but I was keen to get started.

There was no time to lose! I saw this as a six month programme with discernible improvements expected within weeks. So the following Saturday, I hurried over to the hospital at visiting time to initiate my special dementia therapy.

Unfortunately, because the treatment required me to look baffled whenever nonsense was circulating, I spent the entire hour with my face distorted into caricatures of bemusement. It was quite tiring but I was heartened to see Granny closely scrutinising my features as we interacted. I certainly had her full attention, that's for sure.

When I got home, I was of course subjected to sarcastic, mock interest in the efficacy of my programme.

"How did the old dementia cure go today then?"

"No sign of Granny I see. What a shame. We thought you'd be bringing her home with you – completely recovered! Ha-ha-ha!"

"Maybe next week. Ho-ho-ho!"

I tartly reiterated the need for patience and then begged them to bear with my programme for just six months or so. It wasn't too much to ask, surely…

Anyway, the following week for some reason, I had to temporarily abandon my recovery programme.

Due to unforeseen circumstances, I was unable to attend the hospital visit, so my mother and sister went without me. I was looking forward though to getting a full debrief on Granny's progress since the implementation of the therapy. How was she? Any improvement? Any news?

They reported that they'd had a bizarre encounter with the old lady.

Apparently, when they arrived and first saw Mary Bride, they noticed that she'd lost a little weight, looked pale and had an agitated demeanour and lacklustre reactions. It wasn't too concerning but obviously something was troubling her.

After the usual question as to who they were, Granny leaned forward and in a hushed tone, revealed the cause of her anxiety.

"Is Nick all right these days?"

"Yes Mum, I think so."

"Fine Gran. Why d'you ask?"

"Well, last weekend when he came over to see me he looked absolutely demented!"

WHAT?!!! DID YOU HEAR THAT?!!! *That* WAS **NOT** NONSENSE!!!

Even my mother and sister realised the ramifications of this crucial conversation:

"Yeah… we thought she did quite well really."

'QUITE WELL REALLY?!!' It was a double whammy! (as we say in the mental health domain.) Granny's single sentence screamed 'recovery' on so many levels – rational observation, recall and logical deduction to name but a few! Another couple of weeks at this rate and we'll have her back home again!

I tried of course to play down my surprise at my remedy's effectiveness – assuring the others that Granny's improvement was exactly as anticipated and in perfect accord with my expectations.

But blimey, what a result! A few more sessions like that and she'll be discharged – top o' the class!

Another pleasing benefit I noticed at that time was a certain renewed respect present in my dealings with the other two family members… I was definitely held in higher esteem than ever before.

Sadly though, my delight was short-lived.

They reported that Granny's parting shot as they left her at the hospital was:

"Goodbye, then. Oh and look after Nick, won't you? He's famous for his soup."

I abandoned the recovery programme soon after. I could barely boil an egg, never mind make soup.

10

MY SHOUT RON

Ron Vantry, our pianist and singer in 'Mark and the Tempters', 'Soundsa Round' and 'Peter and the Wolves' *knew people* - all manner of entertainers and showbiz types. He worked closely with celebrities every day. After all, Ron had been a sound engineer at IBC recording studios for a good few years and these famous people were simply his work colleagues.

Just once in a while, as a special treat, Ron would grant his friends – the hoi polloi like me – a peep behind the scenes of the wonderful world of professional entertainment.

For example, one day he rang up to see if I'd care to join him at the BBC and actually *appear* in a TV programme.

I was thrilled to be invited of course but Ron explained in advance that it was important not to reveal my humble, non-showbiz status. The last thing he wanted was any embarrassment in front of his superstar colleagues.

I told Ron not to fret. I could easily handle it. He need have no worries that I'd be requesting autographs and the like.

I was going to be playing things cool. *Ultra* cool.

The premise of the show was simple enough.

Ron was quite matey with a very successful songwriting partnership of the time – Doug Flett and Guy Fletcher – the latter of whom was a pianist and singer. They'd actually landed their own show as part of the 'In Concert' series on BBC 2 and they just needed a few 'extras' to populate the set. That's where we came in.

The format of the series was that the subject – in this case Guy Fletcher - would perform a selection of self-penned songs to the live audience, while his adoring fans - in this case Ron and me plus seven or eight other wannabes - would simulate delight and lead the ecstatic applause.

We travelled up to west London one Sunday evening for the recording and, on arriving at the BBC Television Centre, we were directed to the designated studio.

It was a huge hangar of a place with an extravagant-looking set which was designed to accommodate a full orchestra, the centre-piece of which was an elevated, shiny grand piano.

After taking our places on multi-coloured cushions at the feet of Guy Fletcher, or more precisely where his feet would be once he appeared and sat at the piano, we awaited his entrance with mounting excitement.

Oh look here he comes… it's Guy!

"Ron! Guy's here! Look! Here he is!"

No response from Ron. He was playing things even cooler than predicted.

A smattering of applause broke out as people recognised Mr Fletcher. This alerted me to the fact that the live audience for the show was now filing in.

I also noticed that there was a woman amongst us down around the stage area, chatting in turn to each of the anointed 'celebrities on cushions', although she hadn't yet reached Ron and me. The jingling noise of coinage was peppering their conversations.

I'd already decided to take care of the day's expenses – y'know, train tickets, coffees, newspapers and stuff, in return for Ron's generosity in bringing me on the telly and letting me schmooze with his in-crowd pals... oh hang on, she's heading our way!

I gave Ron a quick nudge as the lady jangled towards us with her money pouch.

"Ron, I'll get these, Ron... er... Two please. There we are."

I proffered ten quid.

In response, the woman suddenly discharged a piercing, derisive howl, followed by a needlessly loud riposte.

"Ha-ha-hah-HAH! No-hooh darlin'. WE PAY *YOU*!"

Damn! Exposed! I was stupidly shelling out when I should've been graciously accepting.

What a silly, stupid gaffe! I was absolutely mortified.

I'd fallen foul of the BBC/Equity agreement to pay a fee to anyone appearing in vision... and thanks to live microphones everywhere, my tell-tale blunder was transmitted around the entire studio. (And possibly beyond).

Everyone suddenly knew that there was a fully paid-up hoi polloier somewhere down there near the piano, nestled like a cuckoo amongst the multi-coloured cushions.

Doris of course, the money-pouch lady, was the first person to discover (and reveal) my amateur status – thanks to my bid to pay her an entrance fee, cushion rental charge, call it what you will. She wasted no time in publicising the fact with her raucous laughter. Soon, the whole studio was seeing the funny side.

So, against a soundtrack of mounting guffaws and increasing belly laughs, I attempted an awkward apology to Ron but, by then, he'd moved his cushion nearer the other in-vision celebs and was sighing dejectedly whilst staring fixedly at the floor.

Camera crews were sniggering in surprise, orchestra-members were shrugging, Guy Fletcher was shaking his head in disbelief and I was feeling bilious.

Doris, of course, was still laughing. Loudly.

All right darling, it wasn't that funny.

It was some time before Ron invited me on another showbiz junket, though.

11

EFFING, BLINDING & CO

There's no doubt that the inhabitants of the island of Ireland swear a lot.

They spew out profanities like there's no fucking tomorrow.

In the course of daily conversation, the Irish will fill every available vocal void with a medley of F-word variants.

Sometimes they opt to commence dialogue with a curse – even in advance of deciding exactly what they'd like to say. This is referred to as a 'top', whilst a 'tail' is the term for a profanity-laden *conclusion* to a statement.

Sometimes the Irish just jam in swear words wherever they please. This is referred to as 'willy-nilly jamming'.

As an example, let's consider the following simple statement.

'That car is too expensive for me to buy.'

In the hands of your average Irishman or woman, this straightforward observation could well become:

'Fuck it, that fucking car is too fucking expensive for me to fucking-well fucking buy. Fuck!'

This fabricated example, of course, is a perfect demonstration of a top and tail with random willy-nilly jamming throughout.

Perhaps the most disarming of Irish imprecation though, is when the curse is actually inserted somewhere *within a word* – between the syllables! This form of jamming is the enemy of fluent communication – especially to the ears of a listener whose first language is not English.

I remember being highly amused when a neighbour of ours once warned me that the price of a meal at a certain Killarney restaurant was 'astronomical'.

To maximise the impact of his summation, my friend applied some very basic jamming techniques and ended up with a *seven-syllable* version of the word which perfectly encapsulated his horror at the restaurant's pricing policy.

'Astro-*fucking*-nomical' was his verdict.

Another example of willy-nilly jamming, especially popular amongst devout Catholics, involves the phrase…

'Low and behold.'

This expression is often expanded by simply jamming between the two syllables of 'behold'. The resulting four-syllable word empowers the utterance:

'Lo and be-*fucking*-hold!'

See?

Here's the exclamation given context – as it might be encountered in real life.

'Low and be-*fucking*-hold! That concrete statue of Bono is crying real tears!'

'Well I'll be fucked!'

(Apologies. I couldn't resist a full sentence jam there in the contextual example. It's as if the first speaker has, by dint of his jammed expletive, granted permission for the second speaker to curse. It is of course an invitation that the second speaker is happy to accept and thus the verbal duet begins).

As a second example of willy-nilly seraphic jamming, I offer a short conversation which I overheard recently after a funeral Mass. It took place between two women as they fondly remembered the deceased gentleman they were mourning.

"Oh wasn't he a great man, Bridie."

"A wonderful man. A mighty, mighty man."

"He should've been fucking canonised!"

I observed with some amusement that this could well have been the first time ever that the words 'canonised' and 'fucking' were uttered in the same sentence.

Next, let's study their bollocks.

The Irish have great affinity for this particular word (sometimes spelled bollox) due to its perfect suitability for a wide variety of situations, and regularly use it to convey general dissatisfaction with something or someone.

Example 1. 'It's a bollocks' would be descriptive of a hopeless situation.

Example 2. 'He's a bollocks' would be descriptive of someone with whom all patience has been lost.

Grammatically though of course, these expressions make no sense whatsoever.

Let me break it down for you.

'It's' (singular)

'a' (singular)

'bollocks' (No! This is a plural. It does not belong with the other words in this phrase)

'*It's a bollock*' would be grammatically acceptable but since bollocks are normally presented in pairs, the need to feature the *plural* version of the testicular noun is the overriding influence on subordinate vocabulary.

There follows some examples of corrected bollock curses that can be used with grammatical impunity.

'*It's bollocks*'

'*It's a pair of bollocks*'

'*It's half a pair of bollocks*' (a bollock)

'*It's pure bollocks*' (bollocks with no additives)

'*They're bollocks*' (those people are bollocks)

'*Their bollocks*' (bollocks belonging to them)

'*Acting the bollocks*' (bollock-like behaviour)

Rather than avoid the intricacies of the bollocks/bollox realm altogether, Irish orators wishing to swear profusely whilst maintaining some grammatical integrity, tend to rely on the following standard specimen for most eventualities.

'It's a load of bollocks!'

Sparse but internationally acceptable and dismissive, this five word concoction avoids all grammatical pitfalls and effectively conveys aggressive dissatisfaction – exactly as intended.

'Fuck you!'

Make no mistake though; the F-word is the fallback. It's probably the ideal 'go to' for an Irish rhetorician wishing to rapidly communicate hostile distress.

Often, the F-wording will be twinned with gesticulation (or testiculation as the 'bollock' link dictates). This may or may not involve the middle finger of the right hand. Or, if a push comes to a shove, the left.

Favoured as it is, this pretty universal and dextrous gesture which can be safely executed from behind the wheel of a speeding vehicle is potent with or without commentary.

'Oi!'

This word is the only additional verbalisation that's required. Its inclusion is merely a means of attracting the full attention of the would-be recipient, prior to the insult's activation.

Finally, let's contemplate the curiously unique Irish application of the F-word as an atypical verb.

In most English-speaking territories of the world, the F-word does have sexual connotations. On the Emerald Isle however, it has an additional significance.

When used in its non-sexual context, 'to fuck' means 'to dispose of with gusto.'

Let me illustrate.

Some months ago, I went over to the local rubbish dump near our town in order to discard some household waste and inform myself of new recycling procedures which were about to be introduced there.

Firstly, I deposited six or so black plastic bags of rubbish into the main skip and then returned to the office to pay and discuss the new recycling regime with Council employee Billy.

"So, Billy, how does this new recycling operation work exactly? What do I need to do with my rubbish if I want to recycle?"

Billy was full of information and very eager to share – especially with a punter like me who seemed so keen to comply with the new directive.

"Right, I'll explain. One way is that you buy some eco-sacs – ten euro for eight – I have them over in the office there... and then you just separate your recyclable stuff from the normal waste and put it all into separate sacks – like one for plastics, one for cardboard, cartons, drink-cans and so on. Then you bring the sacks back here, and put them into the relevant containers... over there. Right?"

He waited for my reaction. So I reacted.

"Okay..."

Billy said nothing more and neither did I. He'd definitely implied a *range* of recycling options though. I just wanted to know what that range comprised. It was a perfectly reasonable question.

The silent stand-off persisted but eventually Billy surrendered.

"*Or...*"

"Yes?"

"Just fuck it all into that skip over there."

"Thanks, Billy."

You can probably guess which of his options I went for.

12

OÙ SE TROUVE LA POSTE?

It's only natural for a chap to want to impress his First Proper Girlfriend, isn't it?

Well, when I learned that it was possible to board a ship at the end of Southend pier and a few hours later magically disembark 'on the continent', I decided to invite Valerie, my First Proper Girlfriend, to join me on a romantic two-hour break in Boulogne, France. I was confident that I would impress her as something of an international playboy if all went well. So with her agreement I made the necessary arrangements and soon we were on a little train, clattering down the pier towards the 'Royal Daffodil' which was anchored out there in the middle of the Thames estuary.

I have little memory of the voyage, or indeed the whole 'Boulogne experience' but I'm pretty sure it involved an *omelette*, some *frites* and some walking – that's an *omelette* and *frites each* of course. I was hell-bent on impressing my First Proper Girlfriend regardless of expense.

I think our verdict on the charms of Boulogne-sur-Mer was mixed and as we headed back to join the long queue for the voyage home, I was feeling the need for some giddiness to lift our spirits.

Little did we know, however, that an opportunity for levity (and as a bonus, spontaneous exercise) was about to present itself.

It came in the form of a woman passenger who approached us in the queue as we shuffled slowly towards the ship's gangplank. She had a question.

"Excuse me. You wouldn't happen to know where the post office is, would you?"

I paused. Was this now my chance to perk up our otherwise uneventful day? Certainly. So with a wink at my First Proper Girlfriend, I took the decision to answer the woman's enquiry as if I were a French national. That'd be a good laugh… surely.

So, in response, I hammered our fellow passenger with a succession of meaningless nasal vowels, shrugs and other extravagant gestures. My scant knowledge of the French language was an obvious impediment which risked my detection… but no!

She seemed taken in… and to prove it, she proceeded to pump up the volume and slow down the tempo (as the Brits always seem to do when dealing with foreign Johnnies).

For her second run at it, she took a big gulp of Gallic air and repeated the question, but this time retained only the absolute bare essentials of her query.

"WHERE… POST… OFFICE?"

I answered her re-phrased attempt with some more gibberish and random pointing but she seemed to lose interest and in a surprise move, suddenly produced seven pre-written postcards, which she then plonked into my hand.

"YOU... POST... THESE... PLEASE. *MERCI.*"

I began to protest with more French-sounding drivel – this time featuring a slightly more negative feel but it was too late. She'd gone. Disappeared!

Oh no. My jape had gravely backfired. And now, as the new guardian of these pesky postcards, I felt charged with a compelling obligation to somehow locate Boulogne's nearest post office and sling 'em into its box. All in about 13 minutes MAX!

What a silly, stupid situation I'd created. With no explanation, I elected to abandon Valerie (First Proper Girlfriend) there and then at the departure point, in favour of a risky sprint back towards the *centre de la ville* and probable failure on all kinds of levels. I shouted over at my loyal companion.

"VA-AL! Val! Back in a minute! OK?"

"But... "

As I explained to my First Proper Girlfriend a little later on, 'back in a minute' is just an expression. It was never intended to be an accurate guide as to the precise instant when we'd be reunited. It was said merely to allay any fears Valerie might have had about my missing the boat. Agreed, a minute – sixty seconds, was a highly optimistic estimate of how long it would take me to pinpoint the post office, run to it, lob in the cards and pelt back to the ship... but my point was that it was not meant to be taken literally.

Anyway, I didn't have time for a detailed debate on semantics, so I bolted off instead, wondering if Val truly was 'the one'.

By the time the aforementioned 'minute' had elapsed however, I'd ceased bolting and was by now leaning, gasping and wheezing, having expended all available energy on mad dashing and wild shouting.

"*BUREAU DE POSTE?!*"

"*LA POSTE?!*"

"*QUELLE DIRECTION LA POSTE?!*"

A succession of obliging gesticulators somehow managed to guide me straight to my destination in no time. I rushed up to the letterbox, tossed in the cards and like a boomerang, launched my aching body back from whence it came. I was panting and praying that I'd reach the port in time.

And I did!

Well… just.

When I hurtled breathlessly back into the passenger compound, I could see a single forlorn figure anxiously waiting there at the top of the steps. It was the ship's captain… No I'm joking, of course, it was Valerie. A cacophony of impatient foghorn blasts announced my arrival and the ship's imminent departure. So there was no time to lose.

I was close to collapse as I stumbled up the gangplank, but with Valerie's help I managed to scramble aboard and the 'Royal Daffodil' – a couple of minutes late, (again, that's just an expression) steamed off home to Blighty.

Phew. That was close.

The final act of my exhausting jape of course, was to maintain a seriously low profile during the journey home. For obvious reasons, I was keen to avoid any interaction with fellow-passengers.

My First Proper Girlfriend was not impressed (we're no longer together, by the way).

13

A PACKET OF THREE

I popped into a petrol station supermarket in Kinsale, Co Cork many years back, in search of a cigarette lighter.

I was greeted by a young girl serving alone at the counter and our ensuing conversation went something like this.

"Hi, may I have a cigarette lighter please?"

"Certainly. Three for a euro."

Eh? This took me somewhat by surprise. Why on earth would this service station be offering lighters for sale in bundles of three?

All I needed was a single lighter to light a single cigarette, but as I considered the deal she was presenting, I realised that the proposition was well worth accepting. Her package meant that lighters were exclusively available at just 33.3-recurring cent per unit! Excellent value.

I smiled inwardly at my good fortune, shrugged off all concerns and continued with the transaction.

"Oh, OK. I'll take three then, please. Three for a euro."

"Three lighters? Certainly, Sir."

She disappeared below the counter for a few moments and then resurfaced with some rather disappointing news.

"We've only one."

Wow. Another surprise!

"Well, that's all I wanted in the *first* place! So, as I said, may I buy a, in fact *THE* cigarette lighter? Please."

My exasperation was becoming apparent. It should have been such a simple task to buy a pissy lighter from this bargain basement of a Kinsale kiosk but we seemed to be getting nowhere at all.

At last though, I sensed an impending breakthrough. She now, finally, seemed ready to close the sale. The one lighter in stock was about to be transferred into my possession. She furrowed her brow in concentration and spoke.

"Er... Right."

But no. There was a hiccough. There began a protracted pause as she struggled with the mathematical implications of the intricate financial arrangement she'd engineered.

"Now. So. Em... that's er... that's... that'll be... one lighter, er... um, one euro for er...

Oh we'll say thirty cent."

Thirty cent?!

What a bargain! An additional saving of no less than 0.3-recurring cent!

I was absolutely over the moon!

In Kinsale, it seems, economies of scale do apply, but not as we know them. They're the opposite way around. The fewer items you buy, the less you pay!

Simple.

14

ON THE FLY

Larry Pickles was a great drummer all right but he was even more impressive as a drum packer-upper. After a gig he'd have his whole kit of five drums, cymbals, stool and stands boxed and into his trailer before the rest of us had even got our sweaty stage-shirts off!

We'd hear the roar of a powerful Jaguar engine and see the blurred image of a fancy red car and trailer speeding off into the darkness. Larry had left the building! There was no question of helping anyone else with their gear or shooting the breeze... the man was gone!

This exit policy, which would be referred to by professional roadies as a 'rapid get-out', facilitated Larry's proclivity for a nice, relaxing Cognac at home in front of the fire before bedtime. Reclining in his high-winged easy chair, sinking a tipple or two back at home, was far more appealing to Larry than giving the boys a hand with the heavy gear.

Anyway, this tale centres on a weekend when 'The Retreads' were playing twice. On the Friday we had a rugby club function and on the Saturday we had what turned out to be the best gig of our lives!

We were booked to perform at some awful working men's club in Grays on the Saturday and Larry was the last of us to get there.

Before Larry arrived, Bryan explained to us that in his haste for Cognac the previous night, Larry had inadvertently left his crash cymbal and stand behind at the rugby club. Luckily Bryan, who'd been the last to leave, had found the drum equipment and brought it along to return to Larry.

Bryan had something else with him too. It was the germ of a jape that transformed our entire evening.

He instructed Don, Peter and me to say nothing about the cymbal once its absence was detected. We were to leave the talking to Bryan.

The manager at the club seemed very affable when he came over and introduced himself. His name was Jack and if we needed anything, apparently we just had to ask.

Soon the familiar, throaty roar of a red Jaguar XJS – a blurred one, interrupted our chat.

A-ha. That'll be our stix-man.

Larry unloaded his trailer and we all busied ourselves with the lengthy process of setting up our equipment.

After a while we heard a pained whimper.

"Oh no-oooo!!!"

"What's happened, Larry? What's the matter?

"My crash cymbal! It's gone. *Oh God!*"

There, there, Larry.

"What am I going to do?! And the stand! *And the case!!*"

Don, Peter and I found ourselves grouped around the half-assembled drum kit, offering our sympathy as

Larry mourned his loss. That's about all we *could* do of course, because we'd been sworn to secrecy. What was Bryan planning? And where'd he gone? Our drummer was inconsolable.

"What about this evening?! What am I going to do with no crash? I must have left it at the rugby club last night."

Quite honestly, at this point I was thinking it was time to re-unite Larry with his cherished Paiste Formula 602. He was so distressed, it seemed a bit cruel to spin the jape out further… but of course Bryan had other ideas.

After his short disappearing act, Bryan returned with some promising news for our dejected drumist.

"Larry, I was just talking to Jack the club manager here and he told me they've got a few musical bits and pieces upstairs – including a cymbal. Would that be any use to you?"

A-ha, so that was Bryan's plan. He was about to reintroduce the cymbal to its owner. Not a moment too soon in my opinion.

"Really?! It might be useful, yes Bryan. Where is it? Let me check it out."

"I'll go and get it then. Bring it down and see what you think. Bit o' luck though, isn't it?"

We all agreed that it was very, very fortunate.

A few moments later Bryan returned with Larry's cymbal, packed in Larry's case, ready to be suspended on Larry's cymbal stand.

"There you are Larry. We must put it back when we've finished though, so Jack said."

Larry wasn't listening. He was eagerly opening up his drum case like a kid with a Christmas present.

"Of course I'll put it... Bloody hell look at that!"

"What Larry? What's wrong?"

"Nothing! It's a Paiste Formula 602! Exactly the same as *my* crash cymbal! I don't believe it!"

Neither did we believe it! How could this be happening? Larry didn't recognise his own cymbal!

Nor his own stand!

Nor the scuff-marks on his own drum case!

The scene was set for a monster jape.

Our next idea was to bring the club manager Jack in on the act, to add a bit of credibility to the situation. So after a detailed briefing from Peter, Jack approached the stage and addressed us all. How convincing is he going to be?

He was surprisingly convincing.

"Everyfink all right lads?"

"Yes, thanks Jack."

"I gather you've borrowed some stuff from upstairs... The kazoo, is it?"

Larry corrected him.

"No, just the cymbal actually - and thank you so much for letting us use it."

"No, you're more than welcome. I always tell the bands that come in 'ere they can use any o' that stuff upstairs. There's a piccolo, em a castanet, there's a tuba, a kazoo, three ocarinas and a Jew's 'arp... and the percussion stuff, of course. All I ask is that people put 'em back when they've finished with 'em. It's only fair."

We all nodded in hearty agreement. Larry especially.

By now it was almost time to start playing, but we couldn't resist asking Larry a few ridiculous questions about the tone of his cymbal compared with the tone of Jack's cymbal. He said he felt that in the end, Jack's had the edge - a slightly brighter sound he felt.

But was the stand OK? Was it the right height? It looked a bit short to us, we told him. Larry immediately poo-pooed our concerns.

"It doesn't matter about the height, chaps, it's fully adjustable. Same as mine!"

Oh. So you can adjust the height of a cymbal stand can you Larry? So it can be used by all shapes and sizes. You learn something new every day don't you?

Ladies and gentlemen 'It's The Retreads'!!!

Christ! We're on!

As we played our first song, it became apparent that Larry was road-testing his own cymbal! He was hitting it harder than usual and more often and every time he hit it, one of us would look over with an encouraging nod, a wink, or a smile of approval.

Unfortunately, Larry misread the body language a bit and started whacking the thing on every bloody beat. We had to tell him to spread 'em out a bit... and not so loud.

As we played through our repertoire of songs, I'm sure that minds were not fully focused on matters musical. Our attention was completely taken by the need to expand the silliness beyond all reason. So, during the break, we conspirators had a bit of a confab as to how we should proceed. A decision was made. Bryan should speak to Larry.

So Bryan sneaked into the dressing room for a confidential pow-wow with our percussionist.

"Larry, I'll tell you what... that cymbal you're using tonight sounds very sweet, doesn't it? Lovely tone."

"Yeah, beautiful tone."

"I've been thinking. I reckon we should have it away later on. We can smuggle it out of here 'n they'll never notice. It's miles better than yours isn't it?"

"I know… but the manager was very particular about…"

"Yeah, but we won't be back here again, will we? It's a dump."

"…No. I s'pose not… But…"

Larry seemed uneasy about pilfering his own cymbal but did agree that it was a very tempting proposition.

Bryan left it at that… almost.

"I'll have a quiet word with Don, Larry. He'll sort it."

"No, Bryan!"

Meanwhile in the club, Jack's looking for direction on his next scene in the saga. We said to reinforce the original message whilst looking directly into Larry's eyes.

Which is exactly what Jack did.

"All I ask is that anyfink borrowed from this club is put back as it was. OK? Understand?"

"Oh most certainly." We all concurred in unison.

I presume the furtive conversation with Bryan during the break was weighing heavily on Larry's mind as he solemnly pledged to do the right thing and return the cymbal at the end of the evening.

Hey, we're on again!

The second set was uneventful as the novelty of having found an identical replacement cymbal for Larry wore off. Appreciative glances diminished and soon it was all over.

As we began dismantling the equipment, it was secretly revealed to Larry that Don (the quiet one in the band) was definitely going to purloin the cymbal. Larry looked quite anxious at this news and protested weakly but we told him it was too late. It was out of his hands.

Meanwhile the club manager was just loitering around the stage area making 'don't forget to put it back' noises and, after one such prompt, I mischievously interjected.

"It's a good job you reminded us Jack, about the cymbal, 'cos Larry was talking about thieving it earlier on. Weren't you Larry?"

"*Ha-Ha-Ha-Ha-Ha-Ha-Ha!*" Larry executed a machine-gun laugh of irony and innocence. "The very thought!"

I noticed that he looked a bit pasty though. I concluded that Larry's ashen complexion was probably induced by muted affirmation from Don that the cymbal, stand and case had indeed been successfully nicked from the club and deposited in Larry's trailer.

Where else?

The noose was beginning to tighten around our drummer's neck… and he knew it.

No problem though… as long as we can just get out of here before the larceny is revealed.

Uh-oh, here comes Jack (fresh from another briefing) striding back to the deserted dance floor and he looks pretty damn pissed off. Fuming, actually.

"Right! Wot is going on 'ere then?! I've just bin upstairs to the music room and wot do I find? No cymbal, that's wot! If I told you once, I told you ten bloody times! C'mon, where is it? Where's our cymbal?! Who's got the club cymbal?"

Bryan did his best to contain the manager's rage.

"Just a second, Jack. Calm down a minute please!"

"Don't you give me that, mate! I want our cymbal back. One of yous 'as got it!"

Now it was time for my big speech. I noticed as I winked at Jack, that Larry was keeping a very low profile. He had his back to the action, head down, intensely attending to the task of packing his drums away. No 'rapid get-out' tonight for sure.

Now where was I? Oh yeah.

"Oh I see! So you're accusing us of *stealing* your cymbal are you, Jack? Eh? D'you hear that, Larry? Ridiculous. Absolutely incredible!!"

Larry reacted to my denial with a wan smile followed by a frown of concern as Jack and I circled each other. Voices were raised and it seemed like any minute things could kick off!

My nose and Jack's nose were now about a quarter of an inch apart so I gave him a couple o' pokes on the breast bone for realism plus a cheerful wink for confidence and he backed off a bit.

"Well, somefing's 'appened to it!"

"Yeah, well watch my lips, Jack. We. Do. Not. Steal. Gear. Understand?"

"I'm not saying y'do, mate!"

"Oh yes you are my friend. That's exactly what you're saying! In fact... Right! You're coming with me! Outside. C'mon! Let's all go out!"

Whilst Larry kept his head down, packing away, the rest of us trooped out into the cold night air. Jack obeyed, rather reluctantly, 'cos he was wearing just a thin nylon shirt. I had to drag him the last bit.

"C'mon then, come on! Search the bloody cars Jack! You can start with the drum trailer. Go on, here it is! Do it!" I clenched my teeth for the last couple of words to imply a prelude to fisticuffs.

Whilst Larry continued to diligently pack away his drums, everyone else by now had shuffled outside and was trying to contain laughter. How was Larry going to react?

Now. I threw open the hinged roof of his trailer and there inside of course, was Larry's cymbal, its case and the stand.

"Heughhhhh!" A mock inhalation of air and gasp of shock from Pete, Don, and Bryan.

As if oblivious to the discovery, I continued with my indignant rage.

"So see for yourself Jack! Go on! Take a good look 'n then start apologi…"

My abrupt halt was the point at which Larry must have known he'd been rumbled.

The game was up.

Jack jumped in for the final sarcastic denouement.

Nice and loud Jack. Larry's got to hear this crystal clear! Go on! GO ON!

"OH! WELL WHAT D'YA KNOW, EH!?? Our cymbal 'n stuff is right 'ere in the drum trailer! Wot a surprise eh? Methinks we better 'ave a little parlay wiv the owner of this 'ere red Jag. Where's'e GONE? *Thievin' BASTARD!"*

Fair enough. It was own-up time. Larry's been fingered as a tea-leaf and caught red-handed. Time to face the music. I summoned him from out in the car park.

"Larry… *LARRY!* Step outside a minute will you please? We'd like a word."

There was a pause… and then a desperate shriek as Larry bolted out to face the music.

"No! Don did it! *DON DID IT!!"*

To summarise, Larry had spent a whole evening over-hitting his own cymbal and then apparently conspiring in the theft of his own cymbal and finally shopping his bandmate for kindly stealing his own cymbal.

We didn't know Jack before that night and we haven't met since but we're indebted to him for his generous and important contribution to our silly 'Retreads' jape.

15

FIGHTING CRIME

When I was a jingle-writer and sound producer serving London advertising agencies, one of my very best clients was Ricaldo Spern. He was most loyal to me over the years and we have since become great friends.

Ricaldo and his wife Soosha were the owners of a small advertising agency based in Soho. I'd visit the office a couple of times a month or so to be briefed on imminent jobs and to present creative ideas. The company was located at a three-floor office block in one of the typical narrow streets of the West End.

Recent renovation of the entire building provided identical accommodation on each floor and a common colour scheme throughout.

On my way across town for a meeting there one spring day, I decided that this was a perfect morning for a bit of fun. When I arrived at the downstairs entrance to the building, I pressed 'The Advertising Business' intercom button as I always did.

The familiar voice of Ricaldo's receptionist answered.

"Hello, the Advertising Business."

With no great preparation I blurted out a hastily-prepared address. Inspiration was courtesy of Andy Crawford from Dixon of Dock Green – the way he might have approached it.

"This is Detective Chief Superintendent Colin Franley here from Scotland Yard. Is Mr Spern available please? Mr Ricaldo Spern?"

"Er, I'll check that for you. Hold on please."

As if she didn't know where Ricaldo was! 'Ooh I'll check that for you. Hold on please.'

'Course he was there! Hiding somewhere probably.

…and sweating profusely, I'd wager.

I thought I'd let 'em all stew on the situation for a good while, but eventually I got a bit bored waiting outside - so the next time the front door opened I sprang into action. Urged on by my highly successful intercom bluff, I shot in and galloped up the stairs two at a time!

When I reached the swing doors leading to the Advertising Business reception area, I gave them an almighty kick, burst in and screamed loudly across the reception area.

"NOBODY MOVE! THIS IS A DRUGS RAID!!"

Fortunately, no one seemed to recognise me and although the reception area was quite busy, everyone immediately obeyed my command and stood stock still, looking startled and tense. The Advertising Business staff plainly didn't want any trouble with the law.

Meanwhile, I was scanning the reception area for familiar faces but found none. Surprising, that. And there was nobody grinning over at me with a 'Cor you're a cad Nick' smile, or a 'That was a good one' grin.

Well why would there be? I'd crashed the wrong bloody office, that's why!

I felt very sheepish standing there by the door, as the truth slowly dawned on us all and the day's business calmly resumed. I tried to exchange a few apologetic smiles with people but I had no idea who they were… According to the sign behind the reception desk, I was in the head office of Reinsch IT Solutions.

A storey above me Ricaldo and staff were, of course, still anxiously awaiting DCS Franley's arrival, but he hadn't materialised. They were beginning to think it was a silly prank.

So there I was, marooned on the wrong floor of the right building, with all eyes upon me. *Expectantly* upon me! Some sort of explanation was plainly necessary. And it had better be a good one.

It was the least I could do.

After many attempts, I caught the eye of the Reinsch IT Solutions receptionist, offered a weak smile, cleared my throat and prepared to speak.

Erm.

"Can I help you?"

As explanations go, I knew that this one would always be remembered as… as… well… 'limp' I s'pose, or 'lightweight.'

Anyway. Here goes… again.

"Er, yes er… I wonder if you would direct me please to the offices of The Advertising Business."

"Certainly, sir. It's upstairs – the third floor."

"Oh yes. Thank you. Er, sorry about…"

"No problem sir. Up the stairs and first on the left."

DCS Franley never again made contact with Ricaldo's company, so he was right in the end - it must have been someone larking about.

16

THE 'M' WORDS

You've got to hand it to the Greeks haven't you? Their language is so rich, abundant and descriptive.

Did you know, for example, that Greece's ancient vernacular offers a gamut of no less than three separate variations on the slang word for female private parts?

Each of the nominated options seems to have been invented to precisely conjure up the genitalia in question.

For example, the generic term in Greek (the everyday reference if you like) is the word '*mouni*'. It's selected to suggest a straightforward, standard-issue vagina with no frills and few distinguishing features.

Then, there's '*mounara*' – a word employed to describe a seriously distended growler that has seen a lot of action (too much some would say!).

By contrast though, 'mounakki' – the third option – is what you're likely to hear if the speaker is referring to a fanny that is 'as-new' and in near pristine condition.

Now the reason I'm so informed about all this '*mouni*'

stuff is that I was taught it – tutored by a master – a master of Grecian vulgarity second to none. His name was Helios Pappas. (RIP)

I met Helios for the first time when he welcomed my wife and I to his beautiful apartment complex in western Greece. It rained for two weeks solid during that holiday but we became great friends with the Pappas family and returned year after year for more sunshine, music and indelicacy.

Helios suffered from an obsessional fascination with blatant sexual innuendo, crudeness and depravity of all kinds and his mission seemed to be to convince us of its delights.

Our arrival in Greece - this time accompanied by our two-year-old son Patrick - coincided with a lavish barbeque that the Pappas family was hosting that very evening in their stunning gardens. About thirty locals were expected and it seemed that the Ryans were to be the guests of honour.

As soon as we arrived at the family's apartments, Helios took us aside and explained that he was planning an elaborate practical joke which would keep his guests amused during the meal. Its theme would be, er… sexual.

Might have known.

So the plan was that at some point during the evening, Helios would give me the nod and I was to quietly slip away from the party and wait in the bedroom of our apartment where Patrick was sleeping in his cot.

The apartment was only about twenty metres from the barbeque area outside but we were connected to it by a walkie-talkie system which allowed my wife to monitor Patrick's every breath. She was so paranoid about leaving him alone in the apartment that she operated the device unspeakably loudly. Electrical system noise hissed from its tinny speaker throughout the entire evening... which was nice.

The next part of the joke was the set-up.

Allowing a couple of minutes for me to get to the bedroom, Helios asked for quiet and explained in Greek to his guests that Nick and Sue Ryan, together with their son Patrick, were here in Epirus for a two week holiday. It was amazing to Helios that a young English boy should have such a good grasp of the Greek language.

So that I wouldn't miss my cue, Helios then repeated the salient points in English, aiming to provoke an outburst of laughter that I'd be able to hear from my position in Patrick's bedroom.

"As Patrick make only two years, he sleep now but is poly mature boy for his no-many years and he like to speak Greek words and find beautiful Greekish girl who play poly well the 'clarinet.'"

The laughter that would surely greet the host's grubby euphemism was my prompt to yearn for romance in a high-pitched, infantile voice. My impression would be transmitted to the guests via Sue's walkie-talkie, and their barbeque evening would be enhanced. Once the joke had been executed, we could then return to scoffing the (now lukewarm) main course.

But, as I waited by the walkie-talkie ready to fire, the laughter cue never came.

Oh no, it's all gone wrong! I had no idea when to cry out.

So I waited a few moments and then just ploughed on with the agreed plan.

"*Mounaaaaaaaakki!*"

I hoped to hear tumultuous laughter from the barbeque area but again, there was nothing. I crept back to my seat and surreptitiously checked with my wife.

"Did you hear that?"

"No."

"No? Was it turned on?" Silly question.

"'Course it was turned on!"

Another nod and wink from the host interrupted our hushed exchange. Oh God.

I obediently returned to the apartment and decided on a louder rendition plus a transmitter proximity adjustment. That should help do the trick.

"Mounaaaaaaaaaaaaaaaakki"

Nothing.

So I gave it another go, a bit louder and nearer to the transmitter.

"MounAAAAAAAAAAAAAAAAkki"

Back at our table they were clearing away the plates. I could see them through the apartment window. I started to panic. There goes my chicken! Hopefully I'll get some dessert when I've finally finished entertaining the troops here.

Actually, I felt pretty confident that my second attempt had been successful. Must've been. Strange though, still no one's laughing. Not even tittering.

Back at the table, I consulted my wife for the second time.

"You must've heard that one!"

"No. Did you do it?"

"Course I did it! What's going on here? I'm not doing it ag…"

Yet another nod. Yet another wink.

Oh for Christ's sake! Back I go.

I stomped off in a surly huff, barged into the bedroom and literally screamed.

"*MOUNAAAAAAAAAAAAAAAAAAAAAAAAKKI!!!!*"

I was like a man possessed. All attempts to sound like a two-year-old were abandoned! And they didn't need the walkie-talkie that time either! I was only twenty meters away! They must've heard it through the bloody walls!

I chanced an encore with the generic.

"*MOUOUOUNIIIIIIIIIII!*"

There. May as well chuck 'em all in and be done with it. I bellowed the third!

"*MOUN**AAAAAAAAAAAAAAAAAAARR**RRRAAAAA!!*"

At my rendition of *'mounara'*, Patrick reared up in his cot and started sobbing. My mind wandered to the dessert situation. Better get back to my seat sharpish. Surely I'd earned a nice, sweet, sticky, cakey thing with all this messing about!

I crept back to my (oft-vacated) chair ready for hearty congratulations all round on a superbly executed jape. However, to my surprise, I found the muted, convivial party atmosphere continuing as if nothing had ever happened. I'd given my all but the guests seemed completely oblivious – they were still chatting over drinks and 'desserting' (the verb to eat and enjoy a nice, sweet, sticky Greek cakey thing).

Bewildered by the absence of any reaction, I was keen to discuss the third attempt with my wife but she'd rushed away to console our son.

How could they possibly have failed to hear that last performance? I couldn't understand it.

Suddenly the other guests broke into wild applause and riotous laughter. What was going on? I didn't get the joke and I certainly wasn't going to get the dessert.

Helios was bowing to his guests and occasionally gesturing towards me by now and everyone seemed to be looking over at me and falling about.

Oh! I get it. The joke was at *my* expense, on my good self was it? Slowly the drachma dropped... So everyone here in the garden tonight was in on the joke but me, eh? They'd all heard my ridiculous ranting from the first moment. Yes? Just pretended they hadn't.

Oh what fun! Tee-hee. How amusing.

"Em... Helios, I don't s'pose there's any baklava left is there? That lovely Greek cake I enjoy so much... No?"

Great.

*Malakkas** the lot of you!

*Malakka (noun, informal): a Greek word with a variety of meanings dependent on tone. Mine was aggressive.

17

A BIJOU NITESPOT

A disco is a soulless place by day. It's just not meant to be experienced in natural light. Chinks of grey sky glimpsed through ill-fitting wall panels, dust everywhere, the smell of stale booze and cheap perfume...

Here I was though and it was a first for me. I frequent discos neither by day *nor* by night, but according to my watch it was 4:55 p.m. on a wintry Friday and here I was in the midst of a grand tour of 'The Niche'.

I'd been travelling down to Wicklow from Dublin with a work colleague. He suggested a short diversion to visit Wicklow's newest sensation – a Spanish-style bungalow masquerading as an Irish-style disco!

Yes. Unbelievably, the owner of this bungalow had converted his home-place into a fully functioning disco.

It was situated on a housing estate and I'm calling it 'The Niche' because I honestly can't remember its actual name. I'm calling the proprietor 'Jim Neesh' because I can't remember his name either.

What I do remember about Mr Neesh is that he was given to overstatement – a phrase which itself is something of an understatement.

As my colleague and I walked up the footpath towards the front door of the building (a disco with a footpath leading to a front door?) and rattled the bell-chimes in the porch, (a disco with a porch? And bell chimes?) I wondered if this could possibly be the wrong address.

After a short pause, the door opened and we were greeted by Mr Jim Neesh of The Niche. He ushered us inside.

My colleague did the introductions:

"Jim. Hello. How're you doing? Er… This is Nick Ryan, a friend of mine from London – I thought he might be interested in experiencing your new venture here…"

Wrong.

"Oh. Hello, Nick. Right, OK."

"Would you have a moment or two, just to show Nick and me around the place?"

Shouldn't take too long.

"Yes, certainly. I'd be pleased to. Come in, lads. Mind the milk bottles." (A disco with milk bottles?)

We filed through the door and into the hallway where Jim began his presentation.

"Well, down there's the kitchen, then there's Anna's room. That's our bedroom with the blue door, then the bathroom… and the twins' room is there on the right with the yellow…"

Jim, stop. You're in danger of showing us the typical layout of a standard Spanish-style bungalow! I'm alleged to be interested in the *disco* aspect, not the family living accommodation aspect!

As if he'd heard me, Mr Neesh of The Niche obediently opened the door in front of him and we were transported into the glamorous, sparkly world of disco – or as I'd have called it - his sitting room. It was dark in there – I couldn't get my bearings. Suddenly, a pulsating disco beat was further contributing to my disorientation. The music was issuing from the ceiling - it was deafening and it made me jump out of my skin.

To add even further to my discomfort, there was some shouting going on behind me.

Oh, it's Jim! What's he saying?

"Genwlemem. Wewome oo d' Weech!"

Can't hear him.

"CAN'T HEAR JIM!"

"*GENTLEMEN. WELCOME TO THE NICHE!*"

"Turn down the music! We can't hear you!!"

With some difficulty, Jim eventually managed to wrangle control and calm the music level. He turned it way down to 'intolerable'. Thank God for small mercies. What's he saying now?

"…and finally gentlemen, the piece dee resistonce!"

That sounds mildly interesting, I s'pose…

No, it doesn't!

I tried to appear fascinated as I turned my head away from Jim to stifle a yawn.

"So what is it, Jim, your *pièce de résistance?*"

"Well it's our unique, state-of-the-art lighting system, Nick. It cost a bomb but wait 'til you see it! You're about to experience the biggest disco light show in the country! I'll just turn the music up a bit for the full effect…"

Oh no.

He pressed a button somewhere and immediately the three of us were bathed in a weak green light which flashed in time to Jim's hard sell. Also, some fairy lights became active in the area of what I assumed to be the DJ's corner.

Unfortunately, the impact of the light show on that grey afternoon in Wicklow was severely hampered by the fact that Jim had left the hall door open and daylight was filtering in down the corridor.

As Jim pressed another button, the green colour transformed into white and then gold. (What else but the colours of the Irish flag?)

Classy, eh?

He watched us intently for a reaction. I decided to go for a 'blown away' response:

"Wow, Jim! The tricolour, eh? That's impressive I must say."

"Well, we're pretty pleased with it, so we are."

Goaded on by my bogus delight, Mr Neesh now felt it appropriate to repeat his extravagant claim – this time in italics!

"*Yup... it's number one! The biggest light show in the whole of Ireland!*"

Really? I tried my hardest to appear convinced as I nodded my head in deep appreciation of Jim's claim, but he must have clocked a subtle flicker of scepticism dart across my features.

He decided to qualify his outrageous assertion with:

"*...for its size like.*"

Wonder what the neighbours thought about Jim's size-appropriate venture?

At least it wasn't a semi-detached disco. They're the worst.

18

MUSCLING IN

How did I ever get roped into writing a football song?

To me, football songs are crap. Musically speaking, they offer… (with few exceptions) …nothing.

I have no interest in the game of football and, consequently, had little interest in the proposition once put to me by my work colleague Gary Crooks (RIP).

He was a massive fan of Manchester United – known informally as 'The Reds'. The team had apparently done some good playing recently and scored loads of goals… that sort of thing…

According to Gary, supporters like himself were in the mood to celebrate their team's success! And, more importantly… in the mood to buy anything red or with red connections – especially a recording of a pissy song which happened to be like all the other pissy football songs ever written, but which featured the all-important word 'Red' in its lyrics.

Gary had it all worked out. Our song would be a parody of 'She'll be coming round the mountain when she comes' because that tune is well-known and easy to sing along to. The title was to be 'The Reds Are Back'. Nicely upbeat, triumphant and anthemic. It would blazon the news that Manchester United was, in fact, back and on the up!

On the radio, on the telly - on the up!

At United matches, there'd be huge exposure and we'd no doubt have a massive hit on our hands.

It could not fail. Gary told me so.

"Man U fans will be mad for it, Nick! It's such an opportunity!"

Well, reluctant as I was to collaborate on any such venture, in a flash I reluctantly agreed to collaborate on such a venture. Gary and I spent the best part of half an hour writing 'Red' lyrics to that familiar melody that we all know and love so well and soon, Bob's your uncle, we were ready to roll.

We organised an appointment with a man from the A&R department of EMI Records in London's Manchester Square (an appropriate address for our project) and as luck would have it, he was a Manchester United fan too! Well what d'you know? He was immediately sold on the idea (of course) and booked a studio and musicians to record the music track.

Easy!

Our simple task was to muster and recruit a chorale of (preferably alcoholic) male 'singers' who could hold a tune when wasted... oh and they had to be willing to accept a meagre payment of two cans of lager for services rendered.

Not so easy.

As it turned out, they were NOT willing to perform for a meagre payment of two cans of lager per man.

Things were in danger of turning ugly when, on the day of the recording and after just a single run-through, all the cans had been consumed and the artistes were calling (rather raucously) for more booze!

Two cans per man? Is this some kind of joke? Our Reds choir was apparently looking for an average of nine pints per contributor! So, there was no alternative but to acquire an additional one hundred and twenty pints which were hurriedly procured and finally, apart from some inappropriate giggling, the Master recording was successfully committed to tape.

A few weeks later, the record was released to the team's gigantic fan base.

It sold in the region of twenty-three copies.

Maybe it should be a cricket song next time… or perhaps a croquet anthem.

Now, my pal Gary Crooks – a resident of East Sheen in Surrey - had a nosey neighbour whose imagination had been fired up by all the local talk of song-writing, record releases and top-ten hits. Unbeknown to Gary, something was stirring in the suburbs.

The nosey neighbour's name was Tug Siddley and somehow Tug had discovered that Gary was making waves in showbiz circles with his fabulous football song for The Reds. Tug had heard that it was destined to become a massive Top Ten hit!

So had I, Tug.

Of course the only possible source of this exciting news would have been Gary himself!

It was a boast that Gary would later come to regret.

Although I've never met Tug, I understand that his most distinguishing physical feature was a very narrow strip of forehead 'twixt eyebrows and hairline. He worked for British Telecom at the time and spoke with a nasal whine (a bit like Dudley Moore) which Gary had to endure every evening when Tug popped round for his regular showbiz update.

Tug seemed fascinated with the music business and wanted to talk and talk about the industry. It was almost an obsession with him. Gary was a paraplegic by the way, dependent on a wheelchair for mobility, so he was something of a captive audience for Tug's showbiz ramblings.

It was during one of these visitations of course, that the inevitable happened. Tug arrived with some tremendous news that he couldn't wait to share with Gary.

"Gary, guess what Gary!"

"What's that, Tug?"

"*I've* come up with a song, actually."

As he spoke, he handed hostage Gary a mothy old cassette and a folded scrap of paper on which his lyrics were handwritten.

"It's called 'Julie's Little Toy' and it's quite good. I was wondering if you could get it assessed or something. I know you've got contacts at EMI these days, so you could play it to them 'n see what they think. Might be a winner, Gary!"

"Em… Well, er, yes OK, Tug. Next time I'm at EMI I'll be sure to let them hear it."

Gary of course hadn't heard Tug's song himself at this point, but he placed it in the sideboard drawer for safe-keeping and later attention – a lot later!

He hadn't reckoned on Tug's tenacity though.

The next evening – in fact every evening from then on - that now familiar BT uniform was visible through the frosted glass of Gary's front door.

"Hi Gary. Thought I'd just pop round on my way home. Any news on the song?"

"Erm… well, Tug…"

The news was that, by this point, Gary *had* heard 'Julie's Little Toy' and was determined *not* to play it to the A&R executives at EMI. All credibility was at stake here!

"And by the way, I'm working on another song at the moment, Gary. I think you'll like it."

"Oh really, Tug? That's interesting."

"Yes, it's called 'Come to London'. You can't go wrong with a title like that can you?"

"Er… Probably not, no, Tug."

"So, soon as I've finished it, I'll bring it round 'n you can play that to the EMI boys too… I might come along with you and we can see what they thought of 'Julie's Little Toy'? They're taking their time aren't they?"

"Well quite honestly, Tug…"

"Thanks, Gary. See you tomorrow."

Unfortunately, tomorrow's visit from Tug turned out to be a repeat of today's. It included an update as to the status of 'Come to London', an enquiry about EMI's interest in 'Julie's Little Toy', and not much else.

Gary of course had absolutely no news for Tug, because EMI was ignorant of the man's talents – in fact ignorant of his very existence.

Regardless, the visitations continued. Night after night after night.

Tug was becoming a pest – a self-centred pest. Every

evening he would land at Gary's house for news. It surely wouldn't be long before Tug's second composition was completed, which might then double the frequency of his visits! Oh no! Something had to be done.

Gary tried everything to get Tug off his poor paralysed back… Christmas holidays, staff shortages at EMI, office refurbishment, the Jewish New Year, lack of studio availability, illness in the family, etc., etc.

He was a desperate man!

Such was Gary's distress that he eventually cracked and, without any warning, got *me* involved! He had no shame. He just wanted to be shot of his neighbour.

So at the next update meeting, Gary gave Tug a very positive progress report. Apparently the EMI boys were quite impressed with Tug's song writing.

"Tug, I was speaking to the lads at EMI today, about your song."

"Oh, were you Gary? What did they think? Did they like it? I reckon it could be a big hit."

"Well… er, they seemed to yes, er… they feel you should get a better demo of it done though, and I thought that maybe er… my partner on 'The Reds Are Back', Nick Ryan, he'd be the man to do that for you. You know, a nice new version of it… eh? How would that be?"

"Well… No, Gary, I don't think… erm."

"Just a bit more contemporary, Tug, that's all. He's not going to change it much. Look. Let me ask him. I know he's very busy at the moment but he might be able to do it in the next couple of…"

"Well, there's nothing wrong with my rendition, Gary."

"No-no, they didn't say there was, Tug. They just thought

it might be better to present the song in a more… em y'know professional… er, way. To give it the very best chance of becoming a smash hit!"

The words 'smash' and 'hit' of course were music to Tug's tin ears, so after some deep consideration, he did begrudgingly agree to appoint me as Official Beefer-Upper of 'Julie's Little Toy'.

At this point, of course, I was oblivious to that fact.

A few weeks later, however, I was less oblivious. In fact I found myself masterminding a complete overhauling of Tug's musical masterpiece.

These are our songsmith's extraordinary lyrics. Enjoy.

JULIE'S LITTLE TOY

Always busy at my bench in the shop
'Til the foreman came and said my work must stop
He said he was sorry for one who toiled so hard
It was because the orders were not coming from the yard
It was a stunning blow I really did not know
How at home I'd cope there didn't seem much hope

My wife said don't you worry we've enough to pay the rent
A rest for you and a change might even be God-sent
And there's our dear Julie how she loves you so
Why not make that toy for her you planned so long ago
I tried not to be sad life was not so bad
My wife did understand and Julie held my hand

I gathered myself together and soon made a start
This was a task I relished with a glad heart

The hours that I spent were worth every bit
To see the smile on Julie's face when she cuddled it
My work had been worthwhile my heart was filled with joy
Julie wore a smile Oh how she loved her toy

So, let's explore the turgid opus that was 'Julie's Little Toy'. The original version comprised one-finger piano plus adenoidal whine – both courtesy of Tug himself.

First I changed the tempo and the feel. Then I threw in anything I could lay my hands on… drum machines, bass, keyboards, strings, guitars and brass. When I'd finished the instrumental elements, I then had to sing Tug's ridiculous lyrics and futile melody. I decided on a sort of upbeat 'Cliff and the Shads' treatment and when I'd finished that, to complete the utterly pointless task, I added a second harmony voice – Hank or Bruce style – of which I admit, I was the teeniest bit proud.

So.

Job done.

The irony of it all, of course, was that the boys from EMI were destined never to hear my 'kitchen sink' approach (or indeed any approach) to 'Julie's Little Toy'. I sensed that only the closest of Siddley family members and friends (the latter perhaps in short supply) would be invited to share my unique arrangement of Tug's appalling creation.

I understood from Gary that Tug himself was slightly apprehensive about my production of an 'avant garde' version of his tale of redundancy and its effects on family life.

But never mind.

Once my new version of Tug's song was mixed and complete, Gary was keen for the composer to hear the metamorphosis so Tug was invited (for the first time in his life) round to Gary's house for the audio 'unveiling' of 'Julie's Little Toy' - version 2.0.

Gary's family, neighbours, friends and even members of the press were in attendance at the 'launch' apparently – all eager to experience the born-again ballad.

Next, the 'man of the moment' arrived! Tug walked in to a round of enthusiastic applause. He bashfully chatted with other guests while snacks and drinks were served and then… after about half an hour, the big moment arrived!

Gary, as the host of the event, called for quiet and slowly the babble of conversation abated. Gary then addressed the Tug devotees all crammed into Gary's tiny lounge.

"Well, ladies and gentlemen, thank you for coming here today. It will soon be my pleasure to reveal to you a brand new rendition of the first Tug Siddley song ever written - 'Julie's Little Toy'. We'll be listening and launching this terrific new version and we really hope you enjoy it.

We understand Tug that you haven't heard the new musical arrangement yourself so with no further ado, let's all experience Tug's wonderful revamped version of… 'Julie's Little Toy!' And here it is."

With that, Gary ceremoniously pressed 'Play'.

Now, to his credit, Tug listened attentively throughout but gave nothing away.

Nothing.

As the closing chords of 'Julie's Little Toy' presented themselves and Tug's guests broke into frantic applause at his efforts, everyone (except for myself – I wasn't even present at the Big First Listen) had just one question on their mind.

They were waiting with baited breath... for a sign – a reaction – something. Surely Tug would have at least appreciated all the hours of work I'd put into his no-hoper of a song.

As the last strains of my recording faded into silence, everyone was still looking expectantly at the composer himself for his approval.

Nothing.

Gary broke the awkward silence.

"So Tug, what d'you think?"

"Well that's just shtupid isn't it?"

What?! Bit of a shock from the maestro.

"Sorry, er... Tug?"

"I said that's shtupid, Gary!"

"What's stupid, Tug?"

"Well, I can hear two voices singing my song there, Gary."

"Well... Yes, that's right, Tug – a harmony voice to... er... fill it out a..."

"But that's ridiculous. How can Julie have two fathers?"

For your further delectation, I include a transcript of the lyrics of Tug's proposed follow-up single.

Entitled 'Come to London', it's hilarious and goes exactly like this...

COME TO LONDON
Come to London
Come to London
Come to London town

The Romans and the Normans brought fame to London town
And throughout all the centuries she's gained great renown
There are almost eight million people like me
Now living and working within her boundary

Come to London Come to London
Come to London town

There are palaces, gardens and the home of our dear Queen
Where the guards when they're changing by thousands are seen
There are theatres, cathedrals, churches and towers
There are shops and museums where I ponder for hours

Come to London Come to London
Come to London town

The capital's the centre for so many fine things
It's no wonder the number of tourists it brings
There's so much to draw you on your holiday
When London's your host you'll find London so gay
Now is the time for Big Ben's chime
Come to London You'll love London

Copyright : Tug Siddley

19

DEADLY BUT SILENT

My wife always refers to it as 'trapped wind'... which is a nice venerable term, with a quasi-medical ring to it. I think she uses the word 'trapped' as it tends to endow the function with a veneer of gravitas and decency that the word 'fart' fails to convey.

Call it what you will though, it's a fart – an expulsion of air from one's bottom. And it's hilarious! Ask any male and they'll tell you that there's nothing funnier than flatulence.

Imagine spending a while in the presence of Joseph Pujol, the famous French flatulist. What a hoot that would be, wouldn't it, lads?! The man could fart at will for God's sake! You'd be helpless with laughter for hours on end! Come on, Joe, just a few more *pleeease!* You can do it!

Now, womenfolk don't see the passing of gas in quite the same way, do they? They think that men are being crass and crude when that 'fart-smile' starts to play on male facial features – sometimes with no hint of an audible warning. Within seconds, the uncontrollable laughter always erupts. It just hits the spot somehow, doesn't it, chaps?

'Ooooh I'm so bloated'. That's another one the women use, isn't it?

This innocent-sounding complaint, oft referred to by the ladies, is a euphemism designed to warn of an impending fart, but couched in acceptably delicate terms. The likelihood is that foundations will soon be a-shuddering, but if and when that should happen, let's be clear, the lady is merely a casualty of 'bloatation'.

And there's nothing funny about that, so they tell us!

My wife and I once had a long car journey to undertake. It was from Leigh-on-Sea to Swansea in Wales… via Clifton Hampden in Oxfordshire. A total of around 250 miles.

We'd been invited to a wedding in South Wales which we were attending alone, as children were not welcome.

This aspect of the arrangements complicated our journey somewhat with a detour to drop off our children in Oxfordshire. They'd be spending the night at the home of Sue's parents, who'd kindly agreed to look after them for us.

Another thing that complicated our journey was that I was suffering from a severe case of 'upset tummy' at the time, which as we all know, quickly converts into a severe case of 'upset bottom'.

Within just five minutes of leaving home, I was aware of my debilitating malaise – and so were the other three occupants of the car!

"For God's sake, Nick!"

"Noh, Daddy!"

"Not again! Pleeease Dad."

My 'fart-smile' was understandably present from the word go but I was stoically managing to contain the compulsion to laugh.

Tough ask though!

I 'fart-smiled' all the way to Clifton Hampden where we broke our journey and I broke some more wind. No giggling there though. I was in full control (of the laughter if nothing else!)

After an hour or so in the company of my parents-in-law, it was time to head off for Wales and, as we left, Sue's mother presented us with a lovely selection of homemade sandwiches to eat during the journey. They were beautifully wrapped in tin foil and enclosed in a plastic container.

We thanked her, said goodbye to the kids and Sue's parents and soon enough, the two of us were cruising along the M4, Cymru bound.

Before long, my wife was prising the lid off the plastic container ready to savour an 'on-the-go' picnic.

"Wasn't that kind of Mum to make all these sandwiches for us? D'you want one? There's… em, oh peanut butter and celery. There's cheese, ham… and what's this? Oh, chicken. Lovely. Go on, have a sandwich."

"Er… well, d'you think I should? In my fragile condition, y'know…"

I was still secretly 'fart-smiling' as I appeared to seriously address the gastrointestinal turmoil which by now was persisting well into Wiltshire.

Anyway, I declined the sandwich and we motored on. I was sure that my lower bowel would make its presence felt in due course.

Round about Chipping Sodbury in Gloucestershire, I was feeling ravenous and I must admit that I did succumb to a tasty beef sandwich despite the gas-shifting urges which were still tormenting me.

Big mistake.

Meanwhile, Sue was still waxing lyrical about the freshly-made fodder and the wonderful variety of fillings her mother had come up with.

"Aren't they delicious? Good ol' Mum. She thinks of everything, doesn't she?"

Well they're just sandwiches aren't they? Why's she so obsessed with them?

Soon, we found ourselves approaching Aust Services (as they were then called) near the Severn Bridge. Sue asked me to pull in so that she could answer a call of nature.

I drove to the parking area and she hopped out.

"Won't be a minute. Have another sandwich if you like. There's a lovely sardiney-type filling in those wholemeal ones. Try one of them."

"Yes, dear."

I hate sardines.

She left me alone in the car pondering her fixation.

What a fuss. They're just sandwiches.

I watched her walk over to the main building and disappear inside and then, before too long, she was heading back towards the car again – smiling and waving!

With every step nearer that Sue took, I became overwhelmed by a familiar, gastric urge to release pressure – followed of course, by a need to smile.

Ooh.

No problem... urge resisted.

Bloody sandwiches.

Next thing I knew, I suddenly found myself teetering on that thin line between flatulence and full evacuation.

Which way would it go?

No urge for laughter this time my friends - this is serious stuff.

O-o-o-o-o-o-h.

Accompanied by a gurgle and a tremble, my body tensed with effort and suddenly resolved the unenviable issue. I delivered the most evil, malodorous stench I have ever had the misfortune of experiencing. It was preceded by a sound reminiscent of a child's first attempt at playing a trombone… but louder! The atmosphere in the car was immediately rank – even to me as the perpetrator of the atrocity!

Out in the glorious fresh air meanwhile, Sue was merely paces away from the car with sandwiches on her mind. She gave a brief smile as she arrived and jumped into the passenger seat.

At a glance, she could see the lidless plastic container waiting on the dashboard and she was still peckish. I watched her slowly savour the flavour so to speak.

She was most appreciative.

"Oooh… egg!"

My 'fart-smile' gave me away as the ugly truth dawned.

"Ugh! You *BASTARD!!!*"

I could contain my mirth no longer. I dissolved into noisy, helpless, tearful laughter – it was *so* funny!

Well farts always are… aren't they gentlemen?

20

MY VERY OWN CLIENT

As media planners go, I'm apparently notorious as the worst one that ever set foot in the advertising agency known as Lintas.

I had no comprehension whatsoever of the job that I was employed to do. It certainly involved a lot of tedious statistics, press readership data and television rating interpretation, stuff like that... I knew that the basic objective was to produce a nice marketing plan with recommendations as to how advertising budgets should be allocated for maximum impact but if I'm honest, I never really got to grips with the job.

Apparently our clients' simple objective was to maximise their sales and make loads of money. Can't remember who told me that.

So, unfortunately, this fundamental impediment from which I suffered precluded my being party to any strategic decision-making whatsoever. All the serious stuff was undertaken by my planning-group leader Jamie Curvyn. He was funny, intelligent and exceedingly patient (and still is!).

Now, there came a point during my time in Planning Group One (as we christened ourselves) at which Jamie, in a generous bid to motivate me in my chosen media career, came to the conclusion that I should be rewarded with a client of my very own!

Really??

Yes! I suddenly became the planner responsible for all the media affairs of our agency's baby-food products.

In reality of course, I suddenly became nothing of the sort. I was incapable of becoming that planner. By my 'promotion' we had merely devised an extravagant sham which left poor Jamie doing all the heavy lifting.

The one condition that Jamie imposed upon my 'promotion' was that I should never ever contact my baby food brand manager. If that client chap ever phoned up to speak to me, he was informed that I was 'in a meeting', taking annual leave or off sick. Sometimes he was told I'd 'just popped out for a minute' – a euphemism for locked in the lavatory. On these occasions Jamie always spoke to him and reassuringly explained that 'Nick would be taking action in accordance with the client's instructions as soon as possible'. In due course, a shiny, new media plan from the desk of Jamie (but with my initials on it) would then spew out of the printer for general distribution.

This whole planning ploy was simply an illusion. The reality was that I'd never met nor even spoken to 'my' esteemed client. I couldn't even conjure up the chap's name!

However, things were about to change.

It was late on a Wednesday afternoon, I remember, when Jamie came over to my desk and suddenly announced that I should wear my best bib and tucker the following day.

"Why? What's happening?"

"Your client's coming over. He wants to discuss next year's budgets and have a retrospective look at this year's campaigns."

"Bloody hell!"

"And don't be late. He'll be here at ten. I've organised the big meeting room."

Oh no! My client wants to meet me! In the BIG meeting room!! Why? I was instantly suspicious. That's where all the important meetings occur!

"Look. Jamie. Why don't we just confess that I'm not his media plannering man after all. Tell him there's been a bit of a mix up and... I'm just Jamie's whipping boy. I'll do it if you want! I'll confess that I'm patently incapable of any useful marketing input whatsoever. Just tell him the bloody truth! Eh? Or a joke! Tell him it was a joke!"

No. That wasn't gonna happen. Jamie was adamant that we should maintain the deception and told me to go home early and get some rest. Big day tomorrow, after all.

I had a fitful night's sleep that Wednesday and awoke the next morning, ridiculously early for a ten o'clock meeting in London.

Now... best bib and tucker... erm... My choice was distinctly limited since the only suit I owned at the time was a velvet 'stage' suit – in Dayglo purple. It shimmered under stage lighting and I'd acquired it specifically to enhance 'The New Seekers' Farewell Tour' in which I played a supporting role.

For the Finsbury Park Astoria my suit was perfect. For a media meeting at Lintas - utterly ludicrous.

Before leaving the house for London that Thursday morning, I hauled a bulky duffle coat over my ensemble to minimise its impact on fellow commuters. This of course left purple, spindly legs completely exposed. Not ideal. I left the house under cover of darkness, about ninety minutes earlier than usual. This suited the state of my jangling nerves – not to mention my New Seekers' stage wear.

"Bye Nick! Good luck with your client meeting."

"Thanks Mum. See you tonight."

I arrived at Lintas House at about 8:30 that Thursday morning with the intention of boning up on my client's media affairs - but I didn't even know where the file was kept, so I opted for serious pacing instead.

At about 9:15, the door burst open and in strode Jamie. He was full of energy and ready to go. Ignoring my ridiculous ensemble, he got straight down to business.

"OK, Nick, he's due here at ten. I'll do all the talking. You say nothing. Just look helpful, enthusiastic and eager to please."

It was a straightforward brief but despite its simplicity my jitters persisted. What if my client asks me a question? I'll have to fake a coughing spasm or maybe a fainting fit.

In no time at all, the call came through from reception that my client had *arrived*. Oh God, 10 o'clock already, is it?! Stress can play such havoc with a chap's sense of time.

Jamie went down to meet our man and guided him back to the meeting room. This was the location in which my client and I met for the very first time.

Important as it was… oh, I don't know, but I just wasn't… er… concentrating properly – especially when Jamie announced the client's name. I s'pose it was due to all the tension and anxiety I'd been going through ever since our meeting was scheduled.

I had subconsciously committed a name to memory all right, but it was a name of my own invention and sadly, a far cry from what my client was actually christened.

Yes, I was about to begin a major business meeting with 'my client', having committed an erroneous version of his name to my memory.

Anyway, he greeted me warmly; we shook hands and then the three of us took our seats at the huge meeting room table. Jamie and I sat on one side and the client sat on the other, opposite Jamie.

My boss chaired the meeting – apparently still intent on perpetuating the falsehood that I was the sole instigator of all my client's astute marketing and media proposals.

Soon he was plain lying!

"So what Nick has done for you here, is to consider…"

"Nick felt that the total TV budget was too large…"

"I think Nick has cleverly included duplication stats…"

"Nick has investigated the performance of posters, haven't you, Nick?"

Each and every mention of my name was greeted by the client with a friendly glance over and a smile of cheerful accord.

In response, and in accordance with Jamie's strict instructions, I offered mild return nods and smiles of modesty, twinned with cheery yet focussed sincerity.

It was not an easy role to pull off – especially in a purple velvet suit. However, despite all the potential pitfalls of deceit, things seemed to be going rather well.

As the meeting wore on, I noticed that conversation was slowly moving away from media matters and advertising stuff, to more general subjects like holiday plans, family affairs, the recent warm spell and so on.

It eventually dawned on me that Jamie and my client were by now communicating on subjects to which I *could* make a contribution.

Here at last was my chance to shine… to make some sort of an impression on my phantom client.

I decided that an act of generosity might be a good starting point, so I pulled a pack of Kent cigarettes from my left purple pocket and, with a flamboyant gesticulation which involved rapping the pack with the nails on the fingers of my right hand, I lunged across Jamie towards my client and blurted out…

"Smoke, John?"

These were the first two words I'd articulated since our business meeting began. I was a deaf mute as far as my client was concerned but there I sat in my purple suit, staring expectantly at him for a reply.

He was obviously shocked by my ability to speak English and at the same time, irritated by my bursting into the conversation but his expression turned into a look of disdain as he inspected the white tip of the cigarette I was proffering.

It actually must have been quite difficult to focus on, since a critical lunge misalignment on my part had left it barely a millimetre from the tip of his nose.

Literally looking down his nose, he recoiled slightly.

"Er… No, thank you."

I shrugged, withdrew my offer and lit one up myself. I had an uneasy feeling that my client was scrutinising me as I did so.

Bit embarrassing really.

The two marketing professionals then slowly attempted to rehash the fractured dregs of their dialogue prior to my jarring intrusion.

It's no wonder that Jamie was such a respected manager at the ad agency. In seconds, he'd deftly guided the conversation right back to the world of media, which of course guaranteed my complete silence and averted further humiliation.

I was ignored for the remainder of the meeting but passed the time gazing at the remarkable paint job the maintenance boys had effected on our meeting room.

Time was passing very slowly by this time and just as I was about to ignite a second cigarette, I noticed that my client and Jamie had unexpectedly risen to their feet.

"Well, thank you very much, Jamie. That was jolly useful… em… We must get together in a few weeks… maybe a spot of lunch?"

"Certainly. That would be great."

What? Just the two of them?! All pretence that I'd made a contribution to my client company's success seemed to have been suddenly abandoned! I even sensed a certain coolness from Jamie when I stood up and revealed the full folly of my crushed velvet attire. Yes. Distinctly chilly was the atmosphere. Even my boss – dear, patient Jamie - was evidently irked by something. I had no idea what.

I considered the possibility that our elaborate sham had been rumbled. Well if so… serves 'em right! We should have 'fessed up in the first place. I said that all along. Still… I couldn't exactly pinpoint the cause of the change of atmosphere.

I decided to lighten the ambience with just one more remark – my second of the morning.

"Goodbye."

"Goodbye, Nick. Thank you for all your hard work."

Is he taking the piss? And here comes my third utterance of the morning:

"My pleasure."

Jamie and I then escorted my client back to reception. I noticed that the painters had tarted up the corridors too. Very nice. Clashed with my purple a bit though.

Oh, here we are… we'd reached reception, so Jamie stepped forward to initiate the final farewells.

"Bye then, Alistair."

Alistair?!

Whooo?!

Have a good journey. See you again soon."

Hang on!… who's Alistai…??

Oh *nnnNO-H*!!!!

I could've *sworn* his name was John.

I'm *so* sorry Jamie.

*John – a word with a variety of applications – often used by cockneys as an alternative to 'Pal' or 'Chummy' or 'Sunshine' or 'Squire' etc. Not ideal for the addressing of venerated clients by their advertising agents.

21

GULLIBLE OR WHAT?

I wouldn't generally consider myself to be a naïve or innocent kind of a chap *(Editor's Note: Dad once consulted me earnestly on the merits of replying to a wealthy Nigerian Prince who had made contact with him via email, 'just in case this one actually has the money')* but I must admit that two of my colleagues in 'The Retreads' were very accomplished winder-uppers. Bryan Flater and Don Rickman are their names, and they'd often have me believing all kinds of ridiculous stuff.

For example, they once convinced me that the umbilical hose of a deep-sea diving unit, which links the support team on the water surface to the diver down below, was primarily installed to send him hot soup!

The process, however, wasn't without its problems, my colleagues explained, because the diver's enormous, weighted boots acted as soup traps. The gravitational pull left non-ingested chowder sloshing around inside and risked scalding the diver's unprotected body. This was obviously a Health and Safety hazard and that's why these heavy suits were eventually phased out.

To think that I was persuaded even for an instant by my friends' absurd straight-faced hypotheses peeves me to this very day! How could I have been such a fool?

The lads must have found it so entertaining to know that I could be relied upon to swallow whatever codswallop they cared to invent! I should never have confided in them.

Fair enough, I gladly accepted the concept of nutritious, hot broth being poured down the pipe to a ravenous diver on the seabed below but my prankster pals took things a tad too far with their talk of soup traps!

I was encouraged to believe that the versatile lifeline also facilitated communication between the surface team and the diver, fathoms below.

Now, all these years later, I'm in on the wind-up and I enjoy imagining how those chaotic 'soupy' confabs might have sounded.

"Better shout. Give me the hosepipe. Where's the pipe? *FRA-ANK*! FRANK, CAN YOU HEAR ME?

"WHAT D'YOU MEAN NO?! LOOK... LISTEN. IT'S CREAMY RED PEPPER AND BUTTERNUT SQUASH TODAY OK?? AND SKIPPER SAYS IF YOU DON'T LIKE... WHAT!?"

"RIGHT. GOOD... SO... D'YOU WANT CROUTONS WITH THAT THEN?... WHAT? OH, OKAY. COMING DOWN NOW FRANK. STAND BY!"

"WHAT?... NO!... IT *CAN'T* BE, FRANK!... *IT CANNOT BE, FRANK!* IT'S BEEN IN THE FRIDGE! YEAH... *WHAT?* What's he saying?"

"He says there's too much of it. The suit to soup ratio is way up at eleven D six… and rising!"

"Rising? Is it? WELL TRY AND BLOW IT COOL FRANK!… I SAID *BLOW IT!! LIKE YOU DID ON TUESDAY.*"

"He says no more on his head please. He hasn't got time to duck out the way."

"Right."

"His visor-window's fogging up as well apparently and there's some grated cheese causing problems."

"That must be from last Thursday. Tell him… I'll do it… er… *FRA-ANK* WE'LL DO A TASTY CHILLED MACADAMIA GAZPACHO WITH CURED ASPARAGUS TOMORROW FOR YOU. YEAH? HOW DOES THAT SOUND?"

"NICE 'N COLD? COURSE FRANK! It's his favourite. I SAID IT'S YOUR FAVOU…"

"*FRA-ANK*!! CAN YOU HEAR ME? FRANK!"

It was all very well of course, about the soup and the talking down the hosepipe stuff – I realised pretty quickly that they were pulling my leg about *that*, but nobody ever did properly explain to me how those intrepid diver chaps manage to hold their breath for so long. I couldn't do it.

On another occasion, after a perilous pee right on to an electrical fence, I started fretting about the dangers of receiving electric shocks while bathing in the sea at my favourite spot near Chalkwell railway station.

My fear was that an electric current applied maliciously or in error to, let's say, The Dead Sea bordering Israel, was capable of giving me a nasty jolt miles away in Essex, when I went swimming at Jocelyn's Beach.

Water can conduct electricity all right. I know that much. So why not?

Bryan and Don confirmed that I was right to worry.

So I did… but only for a little while.

Another more minor concern of mine, the flames of which were fanned by my two musical colleagues, was whether slugs could bear grudges.

I know it was stupid but I had this fear that if you were to intentionally harm a slug, it might be able to log the bullying in its rudimentary brain and then lock on and relentlessly follow you – to get even.

I'm bound to have pissed off a good few slugs over the years aren't I? It's likely that we *all* have. They could easily gang up and cause trouble if we didn't watch out. That was my theory.

Fair enough, I was pretty sure I could outrun a slug so I wasn't *that* worried, but I didn't want to be looking over my shoulder all the time in fear of a confrontation with one of these muculent lowlifes.

Also, I was slightly concerned that an astute slug – wronged by me in the past - might well decide to loiter at locations I'd visited before and would likely have cause to go to again. London for example! Or… The Coliseum cinema in Leigh, the Young Catholics Association on Wednesday and Sunday nights at Lourdes Hall, even local shops and the like. Slugs could well be sliming in wait at all these sorts of places – all on high alert for my return.

Don and Bryan immediately latched on to this puerile phobia of mine and explained that if I really wanted to avoid slug retribution, I should definitely keep moving, not return to the same places for long periods of time (Apparently slugs' memories aren't that hot.) Oh and be sure to keep an eye out for any pissed-off looking gastropod molluscs they said.

I don't, though. I didn't fall off the Christmas tree!

I've studied molluscs at close quarters quite a lot and they don't really seem to have facial expressions, so it's quite difficult to assess their mood.

⟋——— GULLIBLE OR WHAT? ———⟍

22

ONE PERSPICACIOUS CHILD

It was going to be a big day for our son Patrick. At the age of just two and a half, he was scheduled for an appointment with a local health visitor which was booked for 10:30 a.m. Its purpose was to give Patrick his first Development Checkup.

Naturally, as parents, we were anxious that he'd do well. We were perhaps even a little competitive in the hope that he was a 'smarter than average' toddler.

The health visitor knocked at the door and entered our house at 10:20 carrying a full plastic bag, a clipboard and some notes. She then asked to be introduced to Patrick. After spending some time gaining his trust, she pulled a set of wooden bricks out of her bag and asked him to build a tower with them. It was a coordination test apparently.

Blimey, this is going to be a piece of cake.

Next she whispered the word 'Patrick' into his left ear and he turned to the left. Then she did the same thing on the right side and he turned to the right.

Done. He'd passed the hearing test!

Wow! Sue and I could have the brightest boy in Southend on our hands!

The final stage of his examination was the reasoning test. The health visitor explained the procedure to us.

"I'm going to check his comprehension and his vocabulary now. I'll be asking him questions which will test the development of his powers of reason."

It sounded like a worryingly analytical test. C'mon Patsy, you can do it.

The health visitor addressed her young charge.

"Now, Patrick, I'm going to ask you some questions. Is that all right?"

"Yeth." (He had a lisp).

"Here's the first one then. Listen carefully and then tell me the answer. OK?

"Yeth."

"If fire is *hot*… ice is…?"

"Cold."

"Very good, Patrick."

Phew. One down. The health visitor smiled and nodded encouragingly at us. She ticked a sheet on her clipboard.

So far, so good.

"Right, Patrick, here's your next question. Are you ready?"

"Yeth."

"If a giraffe is *big*… a mouse is…?"

"Tiny mouse!

"Yes! Tiny! Very good, Patrick."

Another winning smile. Another tick.

"Now, here's the last question. Listen carefully."

I noticed the health visitor's biro was hovering over the clipboard in anticipation of a full house.

"If Mummy… is a *woman*… Daddy is…?"

"A GIT!"

The health visitor and my wife burst out laughing – papers, clipboards and biros flew everywhere! I, as the maligned party in Patrick's summation, found it a good deal less amusing than the others, but crucially I was more concerned that Patrick hadn't given the expected answer.

Could this be a fail?

Oh, give him another chance, Lady, please. He's only little.

The health visitor composed herself and indicated that she was prepared to try again. Oh, thank you. Thank you! He's getting another chance!

Right. Here goes. C'mon Patrick, listen to what the lady is saying to you. Listen.

"Now… really, Patrick, if Mummy is a *woman*… Daddy is…?"

"Really, a git!"

Oh God!

His mother claimed that, whatever his other results, Patrick passed the Infant Astuteness Test with flying colours.

23

TAKE IT EASY NOW

Harry or Arthur or Cyril or maybe Reg was my automotive engineer of choice during the early eighties. I honestly can't remember his name all these years later and have little interest in doing so. Why? 'Cos it's payback time, that's why!

You see… he routinely addressed me as 'Mick'.

Mick Ryan. What an insulting corruption! It's funny how the substitution of one measly little letter in a chap's name can have such a catastrophic impact on its appeal, isn't it?

I seemed to be constantly correcting my mechanic's irritating misnomer (apologies to all you Micks out there), but he was annoyingly incapable of distinguishing between the two neighbouring consonants, which caused all this nominal frustration.

I persevered with him… but alas, nothing ever changed.

Well-stricken in years, Harry (as I'll call him) rented a tiny workshop-cum-botch-shop near the Grand Hotel in Leigh-on-Sea where he attended to all matters motor.

On the upside, Harry was cheap.

On the downside, he was absolutely useless.

I regularly left him – often needing a jump start to do so – well defeated by the intricacies of the very Citroen 2CV which he'd allegedly just serviced.

Unfortunately, in 1983, the introduction of mandatory car seat belts necessitated a specific visit to Harry, his brief being to fit belts in my car and thereby render me compliant with the now obligatory legal edict.

Things were a bit tight at the time as I recall, which goes some way towards explaining why I was back at Harry's at all.

He told me to drop off the car in the morning and collect it, complete with new seat belts, at the end of the working day.

I reminded him to be sure to park it on a slope when he'd finished, on the fairly safe assumption that the inevitable jump start would be required to get me going.

Nine hours after I dropped the car off, I was back on Harry's premises, surveying his handiwork. To be honest, everything looked all right to me – I could see seats and I could see belts. I couldn't properly examine his efforts in the gloom of the botch shop, but as far as I was concerned, it was 'Job done'.

'Job done.' For once maybe even a Harry job *well* done.

If I were a boy scout with a spare sticker, I'd have insisted on adhering it to Harry's grubby jersey right there and then.

"Good man, Harry (or Arthur or Cyril or maybe Reg). Thanks a lot."

"No problem Mick but… er… But…"

"Yes?"

"There's just one… er…"

"Hang on a sec, Harry! Just one what? One what thing? What is it?"

"Well, you know... er... I wouldn't pull 'er up too sharp, Mick, 'f I was you."

Wouldn't pull 'er up too sharp?! The man was talking in riddles! What kind of a caveat was this anyway? It seemed that my trusted motor mechanic was advising me to avoid *any situation which demanded activation of the braking system!*

But *why?*

His mysterious advice left me deeply concerned, of course, but I was so tired I decided to leave it 'til later.

On escaping the oily, fetid ambience of Harry's lair, I took a nice gulp of fresh estuary ozone, got into my car and, as usual, waited for it to pick up momentum on the hill. Once it revved into life, I was going to follow Harry's advice to the letter. Keeping well away from the brake pedal was my priority that evening.

Using the hand-brake alone, I inched my way home where on closer inspection I realised the awful truth of Harry's latest bungle.

He'd only gone and bolted both seat belts directly onto my car's corroded, wafer-thin floor!!

Chassis anchor-points my arse!

So I applied myself that night, alone in my upgraded motor car, to translating Harry's warning into a plan of non-action.

Entitled perhaps; 'The Pitfalls of Braking '

It seemed that any dramatic braking options, were I tempted to employ them, would certainly send my car's driver (namely me) flying through the windscreen at a very high velocity. That seemed to be Harry's main point.

So... what he was trying to tell me was that if ever a potentially fatal head-on collision were to loom large on my horizon, the best course of action would be to select one of his two corrective braking manoeuvres:

1 - 'Feather and die'

Or:

2 - 'Stomp and die'.

You'll notice that the word 'die' is common to both options.

Having just installed the seat belts, Harry of course had a personal preference for the 'feather' option, as it extended the life of both brake pads and driver for a few milli-seconds more.

Harry had warned me of the drawbacks of the stomp approach. They seemed to be mainly monetary penalties. Apparently with 'stomp', I could be looking at the cost of a brand new car floor plus collateral damage… in addition, of course, to substantial funeral expenses.

I made several attempts subsequently to inform Harry that funeral and other end-of-life fees would be implicit in all costings – regardless of my final braking choice -but I don't think he was listening.

"Anyway, thanks a lot, Harry! Nice knowing you.

High time I ventured inside a proper garage."

"Ha ha! Nice one, Mick!"

Actually, now that I think about it, his name was Cyril.

24

ON THE BOHEREEN

Though I say it myself, it was a very shrewd move of mine to get my one-man band business cards reprinted with the words 'For the very best of musical entertainment at your function, book Hozier's bass-player's father.'

And quite honestly, the gigs have been flying in – some nice, juicy ones too! I've even been contemplating a name change to further cash in... er, benefit... sorry, er *salute* Hozier's phenomenal success.

I've got a magnificent mane of chestnut locks on order from an artisan wigmaker in Paris, and some elevated shoes from Milan. Oh, and that name change I'm planning ... well I quite like 'Cosier'.

And I've created it, not in a rip-off sort of a way, but in more of an 'homage' to Andy... a respectful tribute, like. A slightly lucrative respectful tribute, that's it! That's what it is!

I've even composed a few Hozier-type songs for the new act – there's one called 'Shake Me to Church,' er... 'It Might Come Back' is another one (That's my ditty dedicated to the scourge of venereal disease) and 'To Be a Gnome', which is an anthem really, for very, very tall people – like Hozier himself (and indeed *myself*, once I've taken delivery of those Italiano brogues). Again, remember, it's a compliment to his tallness and his voice – it's not as easy as you might think to sing right up there you know, where the air is so rarefied. Both Andy and I find it heavy-going trying to pull those high notes out of literal thin air!

So sure, I'll be performing these numbers 'in the style of Hozier' obviously, but it's going to be very much *my* interpretation. I'm not into carbon copies. I like to be original.

In the meantime though, I'm putting all my energy into touring the bars, clubs, other bars and other… nursing homes actually, around the Kingdom of Kerry with my one-man-banned show.

Life on the road as a musician in Ireland has brought me many amusing observations and conversations but the trouble is that working alone, I've no one with whom to share them. Might be an idea to team up with the man himself, actually. 'Hozier and Cosier'… sounds quite good doesn't it?

Anyway, I digress.

The very first gig I played after moving to Ireland was at a local hotel. Once I'd set up my PA system and was ready to begin, the bar manager came over to brief me on the playing times.

"Right, Nick, start at about a quarter to, a break at half ten, then straight through 'til midnight. OK?"

"Yes, Tom, perfect."

"Good… and take it handy won't you?"

"Sorry?"

"Nice 'n handy!"

"What?"

"Be sure to take it nice and handy."

"You want it taken nice 'n…"

"Yes! *Handy!*"

"Fine, Tom… Handy it is."

"Good man."

I didn't know then and I've never since discovered the precise meaning of the word 'handy' in the context of performing music in public places but I presume that's exactly what I did that night.

So handy that it turned out to be the first of many gigs I played there at the Riversdale Hotel.

The money was certainly handy.

During my early gigs, I soon learned that Irish crowds are most often happiest when entertaining themselves. For this, they merely require the use of a microphone and PA and they're happy as Larry. They're not inclined to piss about with a professional singer.

Why would they? 'Seamus' is in the bar and he has a couple of numbers ready.

"Sure isn't Seamus Harrington a far better singer than this fellah? Get Seamus up!"

"Yes, but people are dancing. Can't we wait? Do it later on?"

Oh no, of course not.

It's always the same. Once the idea of locals entertaining each other is mooted, it *has* to happen there and then. It will go on forever though, as the current singer is directed to call the next 'talent' and so on and so forth.

Now, Seamus and his ilk always expect musical accompaniment on a repertoire of maybe three laments –

they're the only songs they know, they sing them at every public opportunity and all of them are dedicated to a much-beloved female named Mary.

By verse nineteen Mary has usually died and is waiting at the gates of heaven for her admirer to arrive. Verses twenty to twenty-three tend to deal with how much she's missed and there's usually a final request for patience in verse twenty-four, 'cos it won't be long before the loved-up couple are together again in heaven for eternity.

To my constant dismay, there seems to be an unwritten rule on the Irish live music scene that if the likes of Seamus should forget any of the lyrics, (which is highly likely during a twenty-four verse song) he must, at the first sign of a falter, hastily return to the beginning of the tune and start again! This makes for a substantial pause in the evening's proceedings and the local dancing fraternity tends to blame the poor musician for the interminable intrusion.

"Oh 'twas a great night all right but didn't your man let it all fall a bit flat there for a while…"

"Ah sure he did, he did. And he didn't sing any songs about Thompson submachine guns, did he?"

"Not one of them. I'd say old Seamus Harrington could show him a thing or two about singing a good song."

"No better man."

"I wonder does Seamus still do the lessons? He could teach this new boy a few mighty songs, so he could."

Soon after we first came to live in Ireland I was playing one night at a country pub. Following just three songs – each of which went down like a lead balloon – a softly-spoken chap wearing muddy wellies and a Guinness moustache sidled up to me and hissed a command into my ear.

"Let the black sing."

What? I couldn't make head nor tail of what I'd just heard.

"Sorry, what did you say?"

"Let the black... *SING!*" His manner conveyed a certain maniacal desperation.

As he was urging me to take action, I promptly returned to the decoding of his mystery sentence.

Thinking back to my English lessons at school, this inebriated audience member was offering me first, an imperative - 'Let'; a definite article - 'the'; an adjective denoting colour - 'black'; and a second verb - 'sing'.

But I needed a noun. Let the black *what* sing?

'Widow spider' would have worked for me, or let the black 'smith' sing or the black 'and white minstrel' sing…the black 'panther' or the black 'pudding'…even, let the black 'Ku Klux Klan member' sing.

Obviously I could make sense of this man's individual words all right, but once they'd been strung together, his request was rendered simply incomprehensible.

I pondered all possible combinations before shrugging in defeat. Your man remained calm until I finally admitted the unavoidable truth.

"I'm sorry - your request means nothing to me. Whatever you're asking me to do, I have no clue!"

I must admit that I was a little short with our local yokel here, due to the disappointment of my being dismissed from the stage within just ten minutes of my opening number. That's hard on a man.

"LET THE BLACK *SIIIING!*" he commanded. He was no longer softly-spoken.

Luckily, this second version of his instruction was

accompanied by visual prompting and gesticulation. His left hand was indicating the presence of a big fella over by the bar. This man was wearing an elegant black shirt and sporting a magnificent head of thick, white hair.

I wondered, could 'the black' really be 'The Black' – a proper noun? A person named 'The Black'! Was this local perhaps trying to impart to me that the audience had grown tired of my useless, rambling racket and would I ever put an end to the torture of listening to it by inviting a proper singer to take over?

Yeah… maybe it was this person named 'The Black' that the audience was yearning for!

I checked the accuracy of my translation with the man himself and he nodded ferociously with relief, whilst frantically beckoning the… er, 'Black' to approach the stage. No time to lose. Let's get him on. Aha! They hate me! Thanks be to God! At last I finally understood what this audience was craving!

As The Black confidently strode up to redeem my pitiful three song concert and claim my PA, microphone and guitar as his own, the audience erupted with wild applause and enthusiasm.

Soon he was installed in front of my equipment, blasting out through the speakers all manner of mighty music – much to the delight of the gathered locals.

To be fair, The Black was a good singer and was very much the exception that proves the aforementioned rule.

Incidentally, he was apparently christened 'The Black' as a youth, when he sported a wonderful head of jet black hair which slowly turned white with the passing years. Confusingly, it had nothing to do with the colour of his shirt.

To my eternal shame, the next time I encountered my new musical pal, I gave him a powerful handshake and attempted to greet him by name. But what was it? His real name? What *was* that name?

Oh yeah, I've got it; 'The Black'. That's it! His nickname was The Black. What about his real name though?

No idea. Couldn't remember.

I ended up with an unusual salutation;

"Hello, er… The…"

Most Irish pub audiences are generally unable to retain the name of songs. They usually refer to them not by title but by first line. This can make the task of accepting a request quite a lengthy, drawn-out procedure.

I first encountered this trait when an audience member once shambled up to me and started slurring loudly.

It was a slur with a clamorous, demanding ring. I didn't take to it at all.

"Regrets, I've had a few! Regrets, I've had a FEW!"

I could see he'd had a few all right, but was he about to relate his life story or was he merely identifying a favourite tune he'd like me to play? I didn't know and I didn't care.

Whatever his intention, I assumed the latter to be his primary objective but unfortunately, I had no idea which song he wanted me to perform.

Never heard of it, can't sing it. Sorry. Goodbye.

He tottered away a broken man and sadly, this particular drunk on this particular night was destined to forfeit the hearing of his own personal pick of the pops.

Why?

Well, firstly, it was only the next morning that I realised

he had been pleading to hear me sing 'My Way' and was quoting of course, the first line as the title.

Secondly, he was unconscious just a few moments after initiating that special request.

This reminds me of another memorable demand made of me by a dangerous-looking cockney geezer one evening. He wanted to hear... wait for it... 'The Way We Was Once', that elegant Bergman/Hamlisch standard, popularised by Barbra Streisand. It struck me as a rather strange request emanating from a welly-clad audience from the depths of Kerry.

For obvious reasons, I immediately obeyed his intimidating behest and busked a lamentable version of 'The Way We Were' in the hope that he'd overlook my classy grammar and leave me be.

I like to imagine Barbra's unique rendition of the classic song going sumfink like this:-

'Ah-mem-rieees

Loit the caw-nahs of me mind

Misty waw-aahh cullerd mem-rieees

Ovah the waiiiiiy we was once'

Barbra might also do a sterling job on 'Maybe it's because I'm a Londoner' too!

You never know, it could lead to a cockney-themed album project from the diva – perhaps with guest appearances from Tommy Steele, Ray Winstone, Michael Caine, the surviving members of the 'Carry on' franchise...

'If I Was a Rich Bloke',

'Jus' One o' Dem Fings',

'I Can't Give You Nuffink But Love'

...and the ever-popular but technically challenging 5/4 time version of 'Life Is Just a Bowl o' Cherries'.

It goes:

Life is just a fuckin' bowl o' cherries...

There's no shortage of appropriate song titles.

After moving to Ireland, as a family we learned a few local songs so that we could join in a bit at social events in the parish. An amusing example was a raucous, rollicking song which we quickly picked up and enjoyed singing.

The first verse seemed innocent enough but unbeknown to us, the second verse had a bit of a sting in its tail...

'Some say the Devil is dead,

The Devil is dead The Devil is dead,

Some say the Devil is dead and living in Killarney.

More say he rose again,

Rose again rose again,

More say he rose again and...'

People always kind of faded away at this point, leaving the last line unsung. No one ever resolved the tune or the words. Why would that be?

'More say he rose again and...

...joined the British Army'.

Oh dear.

We subsequently dropped it from the family repertoire.

As you can imagine, Karaoke nights are very popular on Erin's Isle (for the reasons explained above).

I remember a big man with a very powerful voice at one such event, belting out a Beatles number. I had him down as the overall winner that night.

However, he fell at the first fence – well, the first chorus.

"She's got a ticket to ri-ide,

She's got a ticket to ri-hi-hide…"

At this point, 'the artiste' unwisely glanced away from the lyrics displayed up on a huge TV screen to give one of the female judges a cheeky 'come hither' wink. It was only a split-second distraction but just long enough for him to lose his place.

"She's got a ricket to tide and she don't care!"

I was right. He won.

25

JACK OF ALL TRADES

I was surprised to hear one evening the following announcement on RTE, which is the state broadcaster here in Ireland.

"And coming up next here on RTE, it's our Sunday film and this week it's… 'Chinatown' starring Jack Nicklaus."

It seems there's no end to this man's talents.

How does he fit it all in?

26

UNDER PRESSURE

Our band, The Retreads, had a very strange relationship with its audience. We regarded them as merely spectators whose primary function was to observe us having a good time – often at their expense. Cues would be missed and entire verses laughed through. Childish giggling prevailed, regardless of the event.

In our band, no opportunity was ever missed to distract or corpse a fellow-musician. Uncontrollable laughter was the single goal and if the audience couldn't dance to it... well, hard cheese, man.

The main perpetrator of all on(and off)-stage tomfoolery was Mr Flater... Bryan Flater, rhythm guitarist and vocalist extraordinaire.

No matter how determined a chap was to make a meaningful effort and contribute to The Retreads' sound, Bryan could be relied upon to bring you to your knees.

I'd see him out of the corner of my eye heading over (or leaning towards me on smaller stages) and it was an immediate: 'Oh no! He's coming!' I'd start laughing in anticipation of what he was going to say or do and it then took only a small nudge 'til I was over the edge and incapable of further contribution.

Of course we all loved music and enjoyed being and playing together, but our overriding objective was fun fun fun – a bit like the Beach Boys. They obviously had the same philosophy.

The penultimate Retreads line-up comprised Pete Brooke on lead guitar, Bryan Flater on rhythm, Don Rickman playing keyboards and my good self on bass guitar. Larry Pickles was our drummer but he informed us one day that it was his immediate wish to retire from music-making. This came as quite a surprise and it meant that we'd have to search for a replacement. Luckily, Larry was prepared to stay on until the new man was rehearsed.

Now Pete Brooke's brother, Dave, used to play the drums years previous. We wondered if he'd be interested in filling the vacant position.

He was.

Pete was confident that his sibling would fit right in – maybe even better than Larry, he thought.

"He's probably a bit rusty all right but I'm sure he'll work hard at it and become a good little drummer."

Well maybe not 'little'…

Unluckily for Dave, who was a solicitor by day, Bryan discovered Dave's natty business suit jacket flung over the back of a chair at a rehearsal one evening and on the pocket lining he spied the manufacturer's sewn-in tag denoting size. It was a single word in Dave's case:

'Portly'.

On glimpsing the size tag, Mr Flater immediately re-christened Dave 'The Big Bonger'. It was probably a nod to another Essex band – a successful one though – called Doctor Feelgood. Their drummer's stage name was 'The Big Figure'. But 'The Big Bonger' was funnier... and portlier.

So Dave made a Herculean effort over the following twelve months and, as his brother prophesied, he became a very solid and capable drummer.

With Larry keen to leave, it was high time we scheduled Larry's last and Dave's very first 'Retread' gig.

Once the date was fixed, the Bonger became obsessed with the song arrangements and his part in them. He was the ultimate professional and wanted to show us that he was the perfect successor to Larry.

No mean feat.

Our new man's debut was set for a booking which we already had in the diary. It was at Westcliff Rugby Club, the perfect venue for a chap's first gig. As an audience, they were a nice bunch of people and not too judgemental.

Good job too!

T.B.B.'s wife would be there to see if all the time he'd invested in music-making was going to bear fruit. Friends, other members of his family, work colleagues... All would be in attendance!

All with ears (and eyes) on Dave.

The night of the gig was soon upon us and at The Bonger's request, he and I arrived an hour earlier than the others so that we could talk through the structure of the thirty or so songs in our set.

He made copious notes to add to his already copious notes and leaked quite a lot of sweat on to them, rendering the majority illegible (he was always a profuse sweater and tended to glisten within minutes of grasping drum sticks, but the nerves on this particular occasion were understandably taking his excretions to the next level). As I sat there with him hunched over his sodden notepad, it was obvious that T.B.B. was succumbing to the imminent pressure of his first live gig in many a year.

After our talk-through, the rest of the lads arrived at the club and we started to set up the equipment. I noticed that Bryan was wearing a woolly scarf around his neck even though the weather outside was benign. He wasn't his normal, sunny self either. Whatever was the problem?

Bryan explained to us all, in a theatrically raspy tone, that he was in fact suffering from a very sore throat. Singing tonight was apparently going to be out of the question. He'd been in bed all day on a strict honey and lemon diet but try as he may, he couldn't shake off the symptoms.

Oh no. Worrying news. How could we perform with no Bryan?

Once Dave was out of earshot, Bryan then confided in the rest of us that he was actually *as right as rain.*

What?!

So what was he planning? I'd been suspicious from the first moment I saw the 'peaky' Bryan that he was up to no good. I guessed that he had a cunning plan in mind and sure enough... he had.

Our opening number at the time was 'Mr Bass Man' – originally recorded by Johnny Cymbal. It was a song featuring two singers. I sang the low 'bom-bo-bo-bom' bit and Bryan sang the lead.

That night of course, due to Bryan's 'indisposition', we were without our main voice, so we had a quick discussion and came up with what we could see as the only feasible solution to our immediate problem.

I approached our rookie drummer and explained that our options were limited.

"Dave, I hate to ask you this favour but er… would you be able to fill in for Bryan tonight? Y'know, sing the opening song for us?"

The Bonger looked absolutely aghast at the suggestion.

"But… but…"

Nobody in the band had ever heard The Bonger sing, so fair enough, it was a high-risk resolution. I addressed him with a sentence designed to turn up the heat a bit.

"Look, Dave, I know you've got a lot on your plate tonight with all the drums and everything and this being your first gig and everything and all those friends and family coming along and everything but we really are up against it here. If you could just sing the first song, you never know, Bryan might be able to… oh, I don't know. It's a very difficult situation…"

The Big Bonger was ashen-faced and silent. The rest of us waited patiently for his response. When it came, I remember it was touchingly obliging.

"Nick. If you think I can do it, I'll give it my best."

"Oh, brilliant Dave! Thank you. I'll go and write out the words for you."

I went away and scribbled a few lines of utterly indecipherable words on one of the sweat-soaked pages of T.B.B.'s notepad, the only legible letters of which were the 'Mr B' at the beginning of each line. As the title of the song, ('Mr Bass Man') it was the one prompt he didn't need!

We reverently placed the pointless lyric-sheet on top of his floor tom-tom, which was set up on his right-hand side.

"Is that OK, Dave? Will you be able to read it all right if it's over there?"

Our visibly shaken drummer (and soon-to-be lead singer) just nodded in terror-stricken affirmation. He had no words.

I must say I disagreed with Dave on that point. The lyric sheet was illegible from *any* angle.

Suddenly, Dave was nowhere to be seen.

Oh. He'd apparently slipped away in the general direction of the gents' toilet.

Time now for his microphone placement.

Brother Peter and bandmate Don had an ideal scheme for this particular aspect of the set up.

Dave was apologetically informed when he finally reappeared that the only spare mic stand we had was exceedingly short, so short in fact that it was necessary to gaffer-tape the stand to a neighbouring dartboard in order to elevate it up towards Dave's mouth.

The mic stand situation was further complicated by the fact that the only spare stand (it being an old piece of kit) had a propensity to droop once it was employed to bear the weight of a microphone. It tended to start moving within just a few seconds of placement. I passed on this minor/major snag to Dave, telling him to 'be careful'. How he dealt with my warning, I never really discovered.

Thanks to our endeavours, we'd actually created a perfectly impossible performing position for our new member's first public appearance. The useless lyric-sheet would be encouraging him to look hard right and the pygmy microphone stand was dictating that he face left… and upwards… and then downwards as it drooped due to gravitational pull.

Our first song would no doubt test all positions.

Dave gingerly clambered in towards his drum stool to try and familiarise himself with our brutal layout.

It was difficult to remain straight-faced as his dangerously contorted neck muscles strained to comply with the assorted demands of this, his one and only Phil Collins impression.

"OK Dave? Close as possible to the mic please, if you can. Are you all right there?"

I could tell Dave was trying hard to answer but nothing sensible was coming out. He was paralysed with fear. We had no idea what he wanted.

"Em… but… Can we? Can we?. erm…"

I looked at my watch.

"Hey! We'd better get moving! I've got to teach Dave the tune yet! How are *you* doing, Bryan?"

The theatrical growl was re-employed to inform us all that Bryan felt much the same as before. A bit feverish.

People were by now starting to file in and some were calling over to The Bonger.

"Good luck, Dave!"

"Hope it all goes well!"

The man of the moment just stared impassively back or nodded. He was by now beyond actual communication. Completely mute, he was in a catatonic state of terror. He just paced the floor, gazing vacantly at Don and Pete as they made further destructive adjustments to his already untenable stage position.

I quietly approached T.B.B. and gently guided him over to Don's piano to start running through the lead voice melody of 'Mr Bass Man'. The vocal gymnastics that I demonstrated to The Bonger bore no resemblance whatsoever to the actual melody of the song – in fact they were totally haphazard notes – but to his credit, Dave did attempt to mimic whatever musical gibberish was slung at him.

I noticed that The Bonger was clutching the sweaty lyric-sheet tightly throughout. A nice professional touch I thought.

Alas, its scrawl offered him no succour.

After his every rendition, I aggressively stabbed a random piano key.

"No, Dave! It's E flat! You're singing B natural. Try it again! No! We're looking for a black American feel here! Detroit, not Lincolnshire!"

Dave realised that I was becoming more and more vexed as he miserably failed to capture the subtleties of my ever-changing executions. Poor Dave.

"No! There's no modulation in this song. I told you before, Dave, it's a *blues* scale!"

I wonder how many drummers are familiar with the blues scale. Not many I'd wager and certainly not The Big Bonger.

Periodically, during our truncated vocal rehearsal, Pete, Don and even the sickly Bryan came over to see how things were progressing. They could risk only short periods by the piano however – it was too perilous to stay longer. We were all in danger of giving the game away with howls of laughter, so I brought proceedings to a swift close – with just a hint of impatience.

"All right, Dave. Look. Just… just do your best. You can't do more than that mate, can you?"

"But… erm…"

"Look at the time. We've got to finish – we're on in a minute. C'mon, we'd better get going!"

"But…"

Dave hadn't uttered anything remotely sensible for quite some time.

It was by now eight fifteen and we were due to start at eight thirty, so we took our places and tuned up, ready to rock. The Big Bonger took a little extra time to settle into the new set-up of course – useless lyric-sheet to hand, microphone droop corrections etc. etc. – and then Don asked him to quickly test his mic. He took a short pause to compose himself and then we heard a distant, alien and trembly voice in the monitor speakers. It was overladen with echo and reverb – a nicely chaotic bonus from Don there.

"Testing-ing-ing 123-3-3-3-3-3-3."

Don was on the verge of cracking up, but he did manage a straight-faced nod of approval before whipping Dave's mic lead out of the vocal amplifier and pushing Bryan's back in.

Lazurus and the Retreads were about to give it plenty… plenty of childish sniggering, that is!

'Constantly disregard the interests of the paying audience'. That was always our motto.

A one – two – a one – two – three – four!

27

THE DUMP

I once received some unsolicited information from an exceedingly drunk woman who'd just been booted out of a local pub. Her name was Deirdre. She'd been making a nuisance of herself inside the bar – swearing loudly and annoying both staff and customers. She then got round to making a nuisance of herself *outside* the bar – protesting at the injustice of her expulsion and continuing to annoy both staff and customers.

As the only teetotaller in the vicinity, I was hurriedly appointed 'designated driver' and ordered to get Deirdre off the premises, pronto! I knew that her home was just down the road, so on that basis I accepted the mission – but quite soon I realised that it wasn't going to be as simple as I'd anticipated.

The first task was to guide Deirdre to my car.

Even though I'd recruited a capable and reasonably sober assistant, what should have been a simple and straightforward manoeuvre was actually noisy, protracted and energy-sapping because our intoxicated charge was struggling hard against intervention.

It was one step forward and two steps back according to my calculations. We pushed and pulled and dragged and cajoled... but progress was sluggish.

Our difficulties were exacerbated by the presence of a small crowd of spectators that had gathered in the car park to cheer Deirdre on in her mission to return to her place at the bar. The crowd was plainly enjoying the entertainment that our tussle was providing.

We tried reasoning with Deirdre but this woman was anxious for more liquor. That was the only thought occupying her mind. (Although it was soon to be displaced by a very different thought.)

So... with great effort, somehow... slowly but surely... my assistant and I began to shuffle her the short distance across the car park to where my rented car was parked. It was a long and arduous operation because the woman was pausing every few moments to vent her spleen at the pub owner and his family, and, of course, to call for more booze.

Finally though, at last we were making some progress.

"C'mon... nearly there... *Deirdre come on!*"

As the three of us teetered the last few steps, with Deirdre in full slur and our audience clapping wildly, I ran ahead to the car, flung open the door and we started to coax, lure, nudge, haul, drag, prod, poke, heave, cram, jostle, and actually force her reluctant carcass into the front passenger seat.

Nearly there. Nearly in...

It was slow and heavy work but at least we were getting somewhere. All seemed to be going according to plan until, to my surprise and dismay, we suddenly encountered *further* resistance from our charge. The woman was suddenly spooked! She hesitated… stared… and then froze!

Our inebriate was ominously silent and immovable.

Oh for God's sake! What now?!

Deirdre's panic-stricken countenance said it all.

"Lads. I've shot my load."

"What??"

OH NO!!!!!!!!

Too late – she was in!

I drove like a maniac the thirty or so yards to her home where we were greeted by her tottering husband who was in exactly the same inebriated condition as his wife.

We turfed Deirdre out onto the damp soil – soil being the operative word – and without our steadying support of course, she slowly toppled over. As she fell to the ground, she exchanged some garbled four-letter insults with her rat-arsed spouse. We left him tending her there, prostrate amongst nettles.

We flung open all the car doors and windows for maximum airflow and then whizzed off into the night.

My mind was spinning frantically as I tried to estimate the likely seepage/leakage factors of women's summer clothing and hire-car upholstery porosity quotients.

How was I ever going to explain away this unsavoury development when I returned to the Hertz car rental desk at Kerry airport the very next morning?

The post-rental inspection was challenging but somehow we got away with it.

Luckily, but no thanks to Deirdre, my motor insurance No Claims Bonus remains intact.

28

DEAD DOG SHOOTS OFF

There were three of us in the car. I was at the wheel, my song-writing partner Bryan Flater in the front passenger seat and 'singer' Peter Davron asleep in the back. The Castlebar Song Contest was over for another year and we were on our way home… Empty-handed as it happens, thanks to our 'singer' and his inability to familiarise himself with our song's lyrics!

Though I do say so myself, Bryan and I had composed a superb Eurovision-style song called 'Touch and Go' which was a finalist in the competition. The carefully crafted lyrics of our opus were trampled upon by Davron and his dysfunction – live on national television no less! He threw in the towel shortly after the first chorus and substituted "La-la-las" for the remaining two and a half minutes of our song's duration!

We didn't stand a chance.

Davron has left the music business now. And not a moment too soon.

Yes, our hopes and dreams were dashed at the Castlebar festival and now here we were, negotiating the barren wastelands of central Ireland, somewhere between Castlebar town and the Rosslare ferry port. We were heading home, defeated.

The repetitious rural landscape was interminable. Drizzle was in the dank air and it was going to be an uncomfortable and protracted journey home. A *wasted* journey, Peter.

The mood was sombre, but Bryan was gamely toying with a song idea for the following year's contest as we sped through the desolate villages of the Irish Midlands.

He cautiously glanced over his shoulder at the lifeless figure slumped in the back seat and whispered to me that we should go for a female performer next time.

Davron didn't stir.

Yeah a female singer sounds like a much better idea Brya-

And that was the last thing I remember before the impact. That's right. The collision!

Suddenly, with no warning, a tatty-looking sheepdog had bolted out from the margin and ricocheted off my car's front wing. The canine missile was propelled high into the air and accompanied its descent with a sustained howl of surprise… and possibly pain. It landed about ten yards from where I'd screeched to a halt and then it scrambled back on to its four paws and was last seen pelting off up the road, presumably in the direction of the local veterinarian.

I got out of the car to examine the bodywork for damage and found a dog-shaped dent on the off-side wing. The indicator light was shattered too.

Bryan surveyed the damage. He knew about cars. He'd renovated an old Jaguar.

"Expensive." Was his one-word evaluation.

As the two of us were examining the destruction, we heard a distant male voice. We couldn't make it out at first, it was so faint.

"Oi-og-i-pilt!"

"D'you hear that Bryan?"

"Moi frog i-filt? What does that mean?"

The words became clearer as the speaker advanced.

"Moy tog is filled!!" Or possibly...

"Moy dog is killt!!"

"I wonder if it's the owner of that dog we didn't kill a few minutes ago?"

Good guess.

A small rotund man in agricultural wellies and a (once yellow) knitted hat on his head suddenly arrived at the scene of the accident. He was huffing and puffing but keen for an altercation.

"My dog is killed! You were going too fast, you were!"

As I was the car owner and driver, I felt a personal responsibility to respond to the charge.

"No. Your dog's not dead. He got up and ran off – right as rain. And by the way, we certainly weren't speeding. I can assure you of that."

"My poooor dog is killed. Shparky's my besht dog!"

"Well why don't you keep Sparky on a leash then, if he's so precious to you? Your dog was unrestrained. And look what he's done to my car! That could've been a very serious accident, you know."

By now, the rumpus had disturbed even Davron and he was sluggishly extricating himself from the rear seat of my car. Fair enough though, once released, he immediately joined the fracas. He fancied himself as a bit of a barrister.

"We were well within the local speed limit but sadly your dog was on the loose and collided with our vehicle. You're liable for the cost of any damage. Simple as that."

Davron once worked in the motor trade so he was pretty convincing.

However, the addition of Peter to the situation seemed to irritate the dog-owner significantly. As a result, the farmer affected a stance of heavy sarcasm, underpinned by the threat of imminent violence. He was directing his fury mainly at Davron who to his credit, never flinched – even when his personal space was invaded by a rural forefinger.

"Oh so t'was *you* driving de car was it? *You're* de big expert round dese parts, eh? De big legal-eagle… De great *know-it-all!* Well thanks be to God you're here to see dat justice is served!"

"Well, sunshine, it's simply a question of funds really – compensation for damage. So if you'd care to give my friend here, let's say 250 pounds cash, we'll be on our way."

"Ya bollocks!"

Peter was warming to his self-appointed role…

"And I suggest you invest in a dog lead at your earliest convenience instead of allowing your canine companion there the freedom of the village. 250 pounds please. Soon as you're ready."

"I'll give you nottin' at all. *Dats* what I'll be givin' you and yer blackguarding friends. *Nottin'*! Now get the hell out of our country *before we blow you up!*"

What?!

We were flabbergasted.

These were the days of regular IRA bomb atrocities in England and this… this was a threat too far!

Time to involve the police.

"Right! We're now going to lodge an official complaint against you at the Garda station. Wait here! We're going to throw the book at you!"

We'd noticed that there was a sleepy-looking Garda station just by the corner, so the three of us marched round, went up to the front door and rang the bell.

We were greeted by an appropriately sleepy-looking guard.

"Lads. Can I help you?"

We gave him a short summary of our troubles – the accident, the fictitious 'dead' dog, the car damage and the IRA threat. The guard was semi-sympathetic but still sleepy.

"Now lads, was this fellah wearing a 'once yellow' woolly hat and wellies by any chance?"

"Yes, correct."

"Ah take no notice of him, that's only Redmond. He's a big tick of a ting!"

As if on cue, Redmond then comes scooting around the corner with the 'dead' dog at his heels!

Davron, who had little to lose in his fast-deteriorating relationship with Redmond, was quick to point out that the farmer's best friend was actually *not* deceased at this stage but alive and 'pawing' (if not kicking).

"Your dog seems to be doing very well after his fatal accident, doesn't he?"

"Ya bollocks!"

"Now Redmond, we'll have a little less language outta you if you don't mind. We need to sort this thing out. These gents are complaining about your behaviour… Your *bad* behaviour Redmond."

"Well dat one dare's a bollocks all right, Denis!"

I had to reluctantly agree with Redmond on that.

Davron *is* a bollocks – particularly when he forgets the lyrics of important and potentially life-changing top ten hit songs – on national TV.

"Now Redmond, these three gentlemen claim that Sparky there ran out onto the road and right into the path of their car. Is that correct? Was he under control by you?"

"He was not…"

Davron couldn't resist another turn of the screw.

"No he certainly *wasn't* under control! He ran right out in front of us!"

"Ya big bolloc…"

"Redmond!"

"Dey were goin' too fast Denis! Wadn't I just heading up the field with Shparky? Out looking for sheep so we were… and… de car was floyin'…"

The Guard was keen to get onto the more serious matter of the IRA threat.

"AND, Redmond… *WHAT'S MORE!!* These three gentlemen, they tell me that you threatened *to blow 'em up!* Is that right?"

"Well…"

"Did you Redmond? Did you tell 'em that? Did you say…"

He consulted his notebook.

"Get the hell out of our country before we blow you up?"

"I did… *NOT!!!*

"Oh. So what *did* you say then, Redmond?"

"I said… er… I said…get de hell out of… our country…
or… or I'll have nottin' to do wit' you!!"

Davron guffawed in Redmond's face and gales of laughter
from the rest of us drowned out the remainder of the man's
robust denial.

"Dat's what I said! Ya bollo………"

"Well, Redmond, 'tis your word against theirs and I'd say
that your very best bet now, the best thing you could possibly
do, is to pay 'em for the damage that Sparky did. Otherwise
it'll mean expensive lawyers and all that stuff."

"But…"

"Come here to me."

The Irish contingent then moved away from the Brits
and continued their conversation in hushed whispers with
the occasional outburst from Redmond.

"But… I did *not!* Dat's a dirty lie!"

Eventually the two of them re-joined the rest of us and
Garda Denis summarised the situation.

"Lads, I've had a word with Redmond and he's decided to
pay you for the damage to the car. Isn't that right, Redmond?
What d'ye think it'll cost?"

Peter snapped back.

"Three hundred at least!"

"Ya bol.!"

"Quiet Redmond!"

"He said two-fifty ten minutes ago!"

Bryan chipped in.

"That was before you threatened to blow us up!"

I interrupted, to avert further turmoil.

"All right, all right. Stop! I'll accept two-fifty for the
damage. That'll probably pay for a new wing."

"There you are Redmond. This gentleman is the owner of the car and he's accepting your payment of 250 pounds. Right? So get his address now and make sure you send that money over to him in England, soon as you can right? Is that understood?"

The Guard gave me a wink.

Redmond looked crestfallen.

"I will, Denis."

Suddenly, with the dispute so easily settled, Redmond had morphed into a new man.

…a completely new man, now clearing his throat.

"Well, lads I'd just like t'say like… dat… it's been a pleasure to meet you. I hope you'll come back an' see us again some day. Have a safe journey home now 'n oi hope you'll be in good time for de boat back t'England."

We couldn't believe it! The transformation was astounding. He came up to each of us in turn and shook us warmly by the hand.

"T'anks lads. Sorry for all de messin'. 'Bye-bye Pete."

'Bye-bye Pete'?! The two of them were sharing a warm embrace! This was inconceivable just twenty minutes earlier. If only we had a camera!

The three of us then piled into the car and fled the village amid much affectionate waving.

'Bye Redmond! 'Bye Denis!

As we accelerated away to make up for lost time, Bryan made a doomy forecast:

"I'd say you've got about as much chance of getting that 250 quid out of Redmond as flying to the moon."

I wouldn't be so sure Bryan.

Back to the monotonous Irish roads, the repetitive landscape and the (now heavy) rain. Davron was soon fast asleep as usual, Mr Flater was planning next year's trip with some girl singer he had in mind and I was back at the wheel.

We reached Rosslare in good time for the sailing, parked the car on the vehicle deck of the boat and repaired to the on-board cafeteria as the vessel steamed its way toward Cymru.

Things were still a tiny bit fractious between production team and performer but we did take consolation for our distress by writing the following message on the sole of one of Davron's shoes while he was deep in sleep.

It was written with indelible felt-tip pen and read:

"My name is Peter Davron and I'm a tosser for forgetting the words to Bryan and Nick's lovely song, 'Touch and Go'. I let them down terribly and I'm very, very sorry".

We wrote the inscription while he snoozed peacefully on one of the bench seats in the café. It gave us some solace. With his feet up on a cafeteria stool, his humble admission was perfectly legible from a couple of yards away.

Tee-hee.

The rest of our journey was uneventful. We dropped Peter off in Bristol and headed back to Southend.

A week or so later, a letter arrived for me with an Irish postmark. Could it be my money? It certainly could. Old Redmond had coughed up!

Good man Redmond! Maybe I *was* going… a bit fast.

Meanwhile, down in Bristol, Davron's father - a vicar - and his mother - a vicar's wife - were still grilling their sleepy son (who'd innocently plonked his feet up on the pouffe for a nice kip) as to the exact meaning of the word 'tosser'.

I understand that Redmond and Peter are still in touch. Y'know… Christmas cards… stuff like that.

29

FOR ONE NIGHT ONLY

It looked like a lovely hotel located there on the banks of the Kenmare River, alongside Ireland's first suspension bridge.

I was on holiday in Ireland with my mother and my sister, tracing distant relations and family connections in the county of Kerry.

We needed a place to stay for the night and the Riversdale Hotel looked to be the perfect spot. We pulled up in the spacious car park and I went in to see if they could accommodate us, while the women waited in the hire-car. It was about 6:30 in the evening and I was concerned that we'd maybe left it a bit late.

I walked in through the main doors to find the place absolutely deserted. Lights were blazing but there was nobody at reception, no guests, no bar staff, no sound… no nothing!

I investigated every doorway leading from the vast reception area but encountered no one. The hotel was warm and bright and welcoming, but apparently abandoned.

It was the Mary Celeste of the hospitality sector.

I then clocked a pair of swing doors leading off from reception that I hadn't checked earlier. I pushed them gently open and peeped into a large lounge and bar area with a massive, roaring fire crackling away at one end. All the tables in the lounge were set for dinner but once again it was bereft of humanity.

Hang on! There is someone! An older gentleman leaning motionless on the ledge of the fireplace.

Was he a member of staff or maybe a customer? I couldn't make it out. He appeared to me as part of a tableau, posing for a photograph – like those you'd find in upmarket countryside magazines.

The elderly fellow scrutinised me as I traipsed across the floor of the lounge but he uttered no words. When I eventually reached him, I smiled and launched my enquiry. It seemed quite important to me that I should, first of all, ascertain the viability of an overnight stay for three people. Especially as the enterprise appeared devoid of staff.

"Good evening."

"How are you."

"Er... Are you... operating as a hotel at the moment?"

I presume that my British accent inwardly enraged the man and prompted a response which combined overt, aggressive sarcasm with an atrocious attempt at an educated English accent. To add insult to injury, he used my exact words.

"Yeahss, we *are... operating as a hotel... at the moment.*"

I ignored his provocative tone.

"Oh great. Well, thank you. May I book two rooms for tonight then please? A single for me and a twin room for my mother and sister. They're just outside waiting in the car."

By this time, our potential host for the night had fully abandoned his smug, piss-taking expression and replaced it with one of abject horror. He went on to explain.

"Oh. Er… well… yes… em no, well, unfortunately we're… we are er… *not* operating as a hotel… at the moment."

"Oh. That's disappointing. Goodnight."

"Goodnight."

Remarkable how things can transmogrify in no time at all.

30

MOSTLY GREEK TO ME

My first visit to Greece was during the month of October 1982 and I went there armed with a single Greek sentence which I had compiled years before, courtesy of my then 'young lady'.

Lia Stylianou (RIP) was a native of Cyprus and my interest in her language and culture was genuine. With Lia's help, I assembled an unusual sentence by chaining together the component words.

After a little practice, I was able to explain to any Greek speaker who'd care to listen, that...

'I want to have the green book tomorrow'.

This was my method.

"Lia, what is 'I want' in Greek?"

"*Thello*."

"And 'to have'?"

"*Nacho*."

"The?"

"*Doh*."

"How about 'green book'?"

"*Prassino vivlio.*"

"Tomorrow?"

"*Avrio.*"

"Thanks."

"*Efharist...*"

"No, I'm saying 'thank you'! For the information!"

"Oh. You're welcome."

So, as I said, courtesty of Lia I was now able to to speak my first ever fluent, Greek sentence – albeit fatuous and with a strong Cypriot accent.

'*Thello nacho doh prassino vivlio avrio*'.

'I want to have the green book tomorrow'.

At the time I had no application for my new linguistic skills but that pointless, silly declaration certainly opened a few doors for us some years later, when Sue and I finally booked a holiday to Epiros in Western Greece. We stayed at some beautiful apartments in a village named Parga.

My Greek sentence was poly-well received by the Greeks because, apparently, green was the colour associated with the social-democratic PASOK party which won a landslide electoral victory in 1981.

So that nonsensical six word statement soon became my party-piece and I'd be regularly called upon by members of the Psoli family, our Greek hosts, to recite it to members of the local community. Reactions always included a congratulatory laugh and the word PASOK.

Once we'd fully discovered the charms of Greece and its people, our family actually spent relentless holidays in Epiros, always as guests of the Psoli family at their beautiful apartment complex just outside the village.

Over the years we became great friends with our hosts and they made every effort to enhance our time in their country. Their generosity even extended to the loan of one of their cars for the duration of our stay! The Psoli family owned a pair of identical small Citroens at the time and one was always reserved for our exclusive use at the beginning of each holiday.

See where my PASOK sentence got us?

Happy days.

One afternoon though, they asked if they could have the car back!

Less happy days.

Bit inconvenient but… s'pose so. If you must.

Apparently four English guests were due to arrive at the apartments that afternoon but were held up in Corfu by a flight delay. They consequently missed the ferry to Igoumenitsa and had to take a small boat from Corfu instead. This subsequently broke down and left them stranded at a godforsaken village named Sivota.

More less happy days.

The last leg of their protracted journey was in an even smaller boat which would be finally reaching Parga's pier at around 10 p.m. They were due to have arrived eight hours earlier at 2! They must have been so tired after all the travelling.

Although it's only a relatively short walk from the pier to the apartments, the Psoli family wanted to make up for the disappointing start to their guests' holiday. The plan was to drive them to their accommodation. So that's why they needed their car back! It was typical of the family's generosity.

Helios, (a non-driver) deputised his wife Lacta to take one Citroen and asked me to drive the other. So in convoy, Lacta and I headed off towards the pier to pick up the new guests and their luggage.

During the short journey down to the port, I hatched a silly plan, designed to utilise my ever-popular Greek sentence and put a smile on weary tourists' faces.

When we got down to the pier, we parked as close as we could to the landing point. After a short wait, we noticed a small craft bobbing up and down on the choppy waves and sailing in our direction. Sure enough, it tied up at the pier and four people disembarked. Lacta and I stepped forward to welcome the two couples.

They looked a bit surly and bedraggled (well, you would, wouldn't you?) but Lacta gave them a warm welcome, sympathised with their troubles and started to carry their bags over to the cars.

It was time to initiate my plan.

I turned to Lacta and without warning gave her a blast of the first word of my special PASOK sentence.

"*Thello!*" [I want!]

She looked startled and stunned but after a pause reacted well.

"Uh… *Neh.*" [Uh… Yes.]

"*Nacho doh! Doh?*" [To have the! The?]

"*Neh!*" [Yes!] She was into it now.

Lacta's English was quite good and she was soon deep in conversation with one of the women about their difficult journey and how tiring it had all been. Lacta was sympathetic of course but had an amused smile on her face as she had been unaware, until now, of the implementation of my silly plan.

"Lacta, *prassino! Prassino!!*" [Lacta, green! Green!!]

Never one to flog a dead horse, I just interrupted a couple more times with random extracts from my sentence, preceded by 'Lacta!' Her reply to me was always the same:

"*Neh!*" [Yes!] Now she was giggling away.

One of the guests then suddenly addressed me as I heaved a large suitcase into my car's boot. He was from 'Oop North' and like all Brits conversing with foreigners, he took it loud and slow.

"CAREFUL... WITH... THAT... ONE... CHUMMY... THERE'S NOWT BUT GLASS... INT... THERE."

Christ, that was a bit of a shock!

"Er, *Prassino. Avrio!*" [Er, Green. Tomorrow!]

He then turned away from me and whispered to his wife: "Not a bloody clue what he's on about."

I decided to hit 'em with the last two words, plus a 'Lacta'.

"*Vivlio avrio!* Lacta! [Book tomorrow! Lacta!]

Lacta was now laughing openly. She did manage her usual "*Neh!*" though.

I was determined to present our guests with my full sentence before we left the pier, so I did that and then delivered every combination I could think of, at high velocity. Sad ones, dramatic ones, and jolly ones. I must say it went down very well – with Lacta anyway.

We were now ready to move off, so we all got into the two little cars – me with three passengers and Lacta with one plus most of the luggage.

To give proceedings an air of local authenticity, I started calling out my sentence to a few random Greek pedestrians from the car window, who greeted my incessant pleas for the green book with a series of confused looks.

As we picked up speed, I felt it was time for a dash of Gringlish.

"So… you was a lilly bit poly lately come, eh?"

One of the women responded. Loud and slow of course.

"OH YES. WE HAVE MANY… PROBLEMS. PLANE. VERY… LATELY… WE TOO TIRED."

"What?"

"AEROPLANE… COME… LATE. NO FERRY BOAT."

"Oh, poly latelyness. Maybe you lose holiday."

"YES. AND… THEN WE MUST… FIND… BOAT. WE TIRED… WE LEAVE OUR HOUSES AT FIVE O'CLOCK… IN MORNING!"

"Poly sheepish I think. Sorry, sleepish. But you are poly lucky can have good look inside of Sivota. I will take you now?"

"NO! WE NO GO SIVOTA NOW. WE GO PARGA!"

"But Sivota is good place. I born there. You make nice tour maybe tomorrow. I give you vairy nice price."

"NO!"

"But never mind… happy holiday can to start here this lately night. You think about Sivota at tomorrow. *Doh?*" [The?]

I took their muted response to be their 'final answer'. They were too tired to argue anyway.

During the ensuing silence, as we got closer and closer to the apartments, I began to fret about just how this masquerade was going to end. In just a few moments' time, my wife and kids were going to celebrate my return to the apartments, in fluent English!

My cover was about to be blown. It was time to explain! But how?

Luckily an opportunity presented itself.

Just around fifty metres from the apartment entrance, there's a hairpin bend which that evening I negotiated far too rapidly – in fact, I barely negotiated it at all! As the little Citroen swung violently around on the corner, I heard an intake of breath coming from the woman sitting behind me.

"Hooooooooooooh God!"

I challenged the jumpy broad.

"What happen? You say 'no like' to crazy Greek driving shit?"

The woman at this point demonstrated another British trait. She started over-laughing hysterically the way embarrassed English people always do when challenged. She was keen to scotch any hint of criticism.

"Oh NO no-no! Ha-ha. Just a little fast… on the bend there. HA-ha-ha!"

It really was high time I put an end to this silliness so I took a deep breath and…

"Well, you may be surprised to learn that I passed my driving test with flying colours in Leigh-on-Sea, Essex, so I'm sure you'll be perfectly safe."

There was a deafening silence in the car. A stunned silence.

My three passengers of course, had me down as a local - born and bred – thanks to my apparent Greek vocabulary and ridiculous foreign accent (but despite my tomato-red complexion).

Their brains were just incapable of accepting the fact that their chauffeur was actually a Brit from Sauffend!

Then again, they were so tired…

Oh, what a long day they'd endured.

A couple of them later saw the funny side but my Northerner pal never spoke to me again during the entire fortnight we were guests at Lacta's Apartments.

Ay-oop.

31

DEEP IN THE WELL

We were on holiday in Ireland.

My wife Sue, Patrick, our oldest son aged four, and Alex, our two-year-old, were heading west.

County Kerry, to where we'd eventually move, was our destination and Gerald and Cherry Kirk were our hosts at their farmhouse B&B near the village of Firies.

We'd stayed with the Kirks many times and they couldn't have been more obliging.

One particular day, we asked Cherry for her advice as to where we might find 'a bit of craic' that evening.

"I'd say you'd have a great night down at 'The Well.'"

The implicit request in our enquiry was to know if Cherry would be willing to babysit our children while we went gallivanting. She kindly agreed to do so. Apparently Gerry would be out at a Community Council meeting that evening, so Cherry was only too happy to watch over Alex and Patrick while she was alone at the farmhouse.

We approached 'The Well' at about nine o'clock that

night and, as we opened the door, we were bombarded by a cacophony of deafening noise – music, shouting, the TV, dancing feet, arguing, laughter, video games and general din.

This was Irish Craic in action. 'The Well' style.

The place was jointed and it was barely possible to get in, never mind sit down. We pushed past dozens and dozens of people.

"Excuse me."

"Sorry."

"Thanks."

"Oops!"

"Hello."

"Oh sorry."

"My fault."

"Thank you."

"Come through."

"Pardon me."

…and eventually reached the bar.

We looked around for a face we might recognise, knowing that there was little chance of finding one amongst all this rural Guinness-fuelled giddiness. We were strangers in town after all.

Hang on! Isn't that Gerry over there in the corner? I thought he was s'posed to be at some meeting…

Sure enough, there staring into space was a slightly dishevelled-looking Gerald.

We gave him a wave.

He gave us a slump.

At some level though, our waves must have penetrated his consciousness (or lack of it) as, with difficulty, he squinted over at us whilst attempting a smile of recognition.

Sadly, his facial muscles were not responding to simple motor messages like that and he was left with just the stare. Hang on! He's hell-bent on coordinated movement now… Look! He's heading this way.

Ten minutes of jostling, staggering and bumping brought him closer and after a further five minutes of people-struggling, he was in our midst.

"I've nine pints taken, an' I'm delighted to… (hic)… see you folksh."

He was delighted to see us all right, because our arrival was the perfect excuse for him to down his tenth pint! He impatiently summoned Pat the barman.

"A pint of Guinnessh and… Sue, what'll you have?"

"Oh, a glass of Guinness please, Gerry, but we won't be staying late 'cos I don't want to leave Cherry too long with the kids."

That was Sue's excuse for avoiding craic overload.

"Ah don't be worrying about her, she'll be absolutely fine, Sue. Abshalooty fi……Shue. No problem in the whole, wide, earthly (hic) world. So that's a glass of Guinness, Pat… and… and…"

Little did Gerald know that even as he tried to speak, back at the homestead our youngest son, Alex, was projectile-vomiting all over any surface within two metres of his cot!

Cherry kindly interrupted the mopping-up operation to phone the pub and relate to the manager some succinct yet disquieting news. He came over to us with a message.

"Gerald, Cherry was on the phone there. She said to tell your guests that Alex has vomited everywhere."

We later discovered that damaged property included bed linen, walls, paintwork… in fact, the entire bedroom had been redecorated in upchuck! Lumpy orange was his choice in terms of shade.

Sue was very concerned of course – she wanted to get back to the farm immediately.

Gerry, however, was completely unperturbed.

"Take your time now... take y'time. Cherry'll be busy wit' the clean-up so there's no point rushin' away. Now Nick what about yourself? What'll you have?"

"Well I'm teetotal, Gerry (a 'Pioneer' as they're called in Ireland) so just a Ballygowan for me, please."

Now.

Although the brand leader in the Irish bottled water market is produced precisely 58.8 kilometres from Gerald's very front door, the word 'Ballygowan' left him confused. Sorry. *More* confused.

The booze, the loud music and the raucous crowd were all taking their toll on Gerry's alcohol-addled brain. He couldn't hear me and he didn't recognise my choice of refreshment. To be fair though, Gerald would know nothing of matters teetotal, so how could he be expected to recognise an alien word like Ballygowan?

Anyway, he tried again. He was intent on supping that tenth pint which was now waiting for him on the counter.

"Nick. What'll you have?"

"A Bally... Gowan please, Gerry."

"A what?"

I raised my voice slightly.

"*A Ballygowan, Gerald!*"

He looked helplessly at Sue. In answer, she shouted it out at him.

"Ballygowan, Gerald, but we must be getting back to

Cherry. We can't leave her dealing with all that mess on her own."

Unfortunately, Sue didn't really have the vocal power to cut through the commotion so Gerald was still bewildered.

Next he turned to the barman for assistance. Coincidentally, Pat was actually pouring out my Ballygowan as Gerald was slurring for assistance. This went unnoticed though, as your man was now completely focussed on guzzling pint number ten.

Annnnd down it went.

He wiped the froth from his lips with the back of his hand and tenaciously re-commenced his interrogation.

"Ah, go on. What ish it Pat? What'sh-he…(hic) watsee want?"

"A Ballygowan, Gerry. And he has it there in front of him. Look!"

Gerry looked… wasted… and addled.

"Nick. What do y'want to *drink*… for (hic) God'shake man?!"

I gave it one last, resounding belt.

"A BALLYGOWAN Gerry!! ***BALLY – GOWAN !!!!***"

"Yes Nick, I know… but a Bally *GALLON OF WHAT*??!"

Here we go again.

How in the name of God did Gerry think I could down eight imperial pints of any drink?

32

SHE MAY GET OUT OF IT YET

I hadn't seen Dan for a good while but there he was ambling down Main Street coming straight towards me.

Any second we'd be colliding on the pavement and in for a big chat. I was slightly reticent about the impending exchange however, because it was bound to include an update on the health status of Dan's elderly parents – one of whom had recently been quite ill. That much I knew, but I couldn't for the life of me remember which one of his parents had been poorly. Who was it? His mother or his father?

With every step I was wracking my brains... but I simply could not remember. Which parent? It'd be awful to flaunt my ignorance of his family's well-being with a crass enquiry.

Uh-oh. He's seen me.

"Nick! How's things?"

I greeted him and we shook hands.

"Hello Dan. How are you doing? Haven't seen you since before Christmas..."

I find the only course of action in these situations is to chat generally and trust that the facts will eventually reveal themselves as the conversation progresses.

"Busy these days, Dan?"

"Well, you know yourself."

"I do yeah. So... are you heading into town on the fifteenth for fair day or...?"

"Well... I may and I mayn't."

"Let's hope we get the weather for it this year. Some rain last night, wasn't it?"

"Mighty rain all right, Nick."

"Er... is your brother still...?" Sadly I didn't have enough information to complete this particular enquiry – why ever did I start it? I wasn't even sure if this man *had* a brother! Fortunately, he did, so Dan kindly completed my half-baked query for me.

"...still over in Cork? Oh God yeah."

I nodded a nod of serious comprehension.

"Right."

In the silence that followed, I realised that my reference to Dan's brother was a very unwise move, because it opened up our dialogue to include Dan's other family members – like his mother and father, for example.

My plan was failing miserably. Our dialogue was more like an interview than a conversation. I was asking questions and Dan was replying with monosyllabic answers! Consequently, ten minutes into our chat I was still clueless as to which one of his bloody parents was under the weather... so I considered my options. There was a fifty-fifty chance of getting it wrong (and/or right).

Risky.

Avoidance was my first impulse so I patted him on the shoulder in a gesture of conclusion.

"Oh well, Dan, I'd better let you go. Nice to see you. 'Bye."

"Good luck, Nick."

We continued on our separate ways for a few seconds but after a couple of paces, I found myself stopping, turning and bellowing.

"Oh, by the way, Dan…"

"Yes, Nick?"

"How's your… er… (so far so good) … Mum?"

"She's dead at the moment."

Thought so.

It was his mother then.

33

IN PRAISE OF THE
FEMALE FORM

My guess is that my mother always suspected I was hovering somewhere over on the gay side. In truth, I was merely a repressed Catholic and dangerously timid to boot!

My mother was very funny. Sometimes you'd be laughing with her and other times you'd be laughing *at* her. This little story demonstrates an example of the latter.

At the age of 18, I had met and befriended a French pen pal named Marie-Christiane Beaudoux with whom I regularly corresponded. She demonstrated no knowledge of English so we'd write to each other in French, of which I had just a smattering of words and a sprinkling of grammar.

Our family had encountered my future penfriend back in 1964 during a camping holiday in the Schwartzwald.

You'd hardly call my relationship with Marie-Christiane a romantic liaison – partly because I was a bit slow on the old amorous uptake thanks to my papist rearing, and partly because every affectionate gesture I ever offered the mademoiselle was resolutely rejected.

What a conundrum it was.

Ultimately, my romantic tempo was apparently too rapid for Marie-Christiane yet far too leisurely for my mother, who evidently assumed me to be a committed nancy-boy in the making - a son in urgent need of salvation.

Rather than confronting me with her suspicions however, my mother had plainly decided that the best course of action was to 'talk me out' of my deviant tendency. Her approach would be one of distraction and realignment, one I'd hardly even notice was happening.

Of course I *did* notice it was happening. In fact it became rather tedious. Once this pen pal business had been re-established, my mother really layered on the encouragement of my international liaison. In fact, every sentence that she uttered risked the inclusion of a Marie-Christiane reference or hint.

"Any news from Marie-Christiane, Nick?"

"I wonder what the weather's like over there in France."

"Nick, what's the French for 'Get stuck in'?"

"You'd better reply to Marie-Christiane's letter, hadn't you?"

My pen pal of course knew nothing of my mother's Cupidic aspirations and we continued to maintain our postual, textual (but unfortunately not sextual) relationship.

A year or so into our correspondence, my mother organised a camping holiday for the three of us –herself, my sister and me – to Sitges in Spain, which involved driving from Calais down through France to the Spanish coast south of Barcelona.

When she consulted the map, my mother noticed that the route led us through Chateaudun and Blois – two French towns quite close to the village of La Ferte Villeneuil in which my pen pal's family lived. My mother kindly suggested that it was the perfect opportunity for the pen pals to meet again. I was up for it, my sister was reasonably up for it, but my mother was *earnestly* up for it - so the holiday schedule was amended to incorporate my mother's diversion. (In French the word would be '*deviation*', funnily enough)

On the eve of our visit to the Beaudoux farm, we were forced to spend the night sleeping out under the stars. This was due to a hotel booking cock-up (or should that be coq-up?) which left us with nowhere to stay but our sleeping bags. Thankfully the weather was benign, but the mistake resulted in three dishevelled Brits appearing (unannounced) on the Beaudoux family's doorstep for breakfast! At the outrageous hour of 8:30 a.m.! Whatever possessed us?!

La Famille Beaudoux was half-dressed and panicking at our arrival. Sleepy faces peered out at us through every window as they tried to identify the perpetrators of this untimely visitation.

We tried shouting that we were no threat to the family's safety but the heavy front door and our limited linguistic skills conspired to complicate the message, and actually render it void.

Eventually, following a long struggle with the internal locking mechanism of the front door, it was swung slowly open to reveal Monsieur Beaudoux – the father of my pen pal and mayor of La Ferte Villeneuil. The door was plainly considered a task for the 'man of the house'. He looked a little apprehensive as we spoke and he narrowed his eyes for maximum comprehension of our appalling accents. My sister had the best French so she began the clarification and as she started her speech, Marie-Christiane appeared.

175

"Quelle surprise! Quel plaisir!"

She explained to her family who we were and hastily appointed herself our guide – whisking us off (surely at the suggestion of other Beaudoux) for a tour of the village and the numerous fields of maize for which her family was responsible.

One would assume that the tour was instigated at the behest of Marie-Christiane's mother, who may well have wished that the grass-stained, *'deputation Anglaise'* had delayed its visit by six hours or so.

Conversation on the grand tour was stilted - our ignorance of each other's mother tongue made communication quite challenging. We walked up and down the main street several times and then embarked on a crop inspection.

Towards the end of the tour, we found ourselves in a maize field where there was another momentary lull in the conversation.

My mother saw her chance and snuck in to claim the gap. With a nod towards my pen pal and a pretend scratch of her nose to distract from her impending observation, she addressed me from the side of her mouth.

"Nice little titties."

Pause of astonishment all round.

Oh my God. Was that my mother speaking before this deafening silence?! Who's going to follow that?

Marie-Christiane of course.

First, a coy smile. And then…

"Oh, merci beaucoup, Madame Ryan."

She did have a bit of English then…

Oh Mum.

34

DENTAL ON MY MIND

It was a familiar location to me, that room... a waiting area in which I'd nervously paced once before. In fact, almost precisely a year before.

I was back at Guy's Dental Hospital in London for a second attempt at securing a place there as a dental student.

One year earlier, I'd been offered a place at the world-renowned teaching hospital and now, having failed miserably to pass two of the three relevant G.C.E. examinations, I was back for more.

My previous application had been successful, due in part, I felt, to my cunning responses to some key questions put to me by the Dean of Dental Studies and his selection team.

I remember the Dean peering at me over his half-moon spectacles as he enquired as to my eventual career path.

"Now, Nicholas. In which particular branch of dental medicine would you like to specialise once you've qualified?"

"Oh, children's dentistry I think, sir. I seem to have a natural connection with youngsters. You know… putting them at ease and…"

Result!

Smiles all round. The selection panel had suddenly morphed into three Cheshire cats at this news. They were now grinning over at me whilst scribbling copious notes (an impossible feat you may say but it's true!).

Actually, I happened to discover that there was a shortage of kids' dentists that very morning, because I'd travelled to London with a dentist friend of mine and she'd given me the lowdown. Apparently no one was interested in treating damn children with their tiny mouths, low pain thresholds and pissy treatment plans.

The big money was in implants, orthodontics and rampant decay. Ironically the direction in which my career path would soon be heading!

Ah. They've stopped scrawling. Come on. Next question. I'm feeling lucky… punk!

"And tell us Nicholas, why Guy's? Why do you wish to study here at Guy's Dental Hospital?"

"Well, sir, I believe Guy's to be the best teaching hospital in the world… and I will *need* the best of teaching! Ha-hah."

"Ho-hah!" They were laughing out loud now. It was going so well I even threw in a little extra witticism.

"I'm just that type of Guy… sir."

Get it? Guy… Guys. You may, but I don't believe they did.

Anyway, they offered me a place at their la-de-dah hospital which was very nice of them, but it was conditional upon my attaining three 'Grade E' passes (the very lowest of the low) in chemistry, physics and biology. Piece of cake, I thought… yeah. No problem.

Alas, my lamentable exam results did present a few problems. They rendered me impotent in my quest to benefit from all that Guy's tip-top training. I achieved one D and two Fs… That's F for 'Fail', of course.

But that was last year! Now I'm back again in that same waiting room ready for a second bash, twelve months older, twelve months wiser. Surely this re-interview they're insisting on is a mere formality. They'd already accepted me a year earlier. *Thrilled* they were to welcome me aboard last year, so… I mean, I've still got the letter. I should've brought it as proof.

As I pushed open the door, I noticed that the waiting room was much busier this time than it was the previous February – crammed with eager-beaver dental 'students-to-be', all jostling for one of the limited places on offer.

I got chatting with a few of them and related my previous experience of inquisition by the 'Dean team'. I quickly became the old sage of the dental school selection queue, holding court and dispensing nuggets of useful advice and tips on interview techniques.

'Why?' I later wondered. After all, these people were my competitors.

My competitors seemed very appreciative of all the advice I was sharing on how to handle a dental hospital interview but one by one, names were being called and the waiting room population was diminishing. I'd befriended a young lad named Michael by this stage who listened intently to my words of wisdom, until eventually he was called and I was left alone, listening out for…

"Mr Ryan?"

I was desperate to let everyone and anyone know that I was an 'old hand' at this interview lark. Get 'em on my side sort of thing. I'll start with her – that young receptionist girl there.

"Mr Nicholas Ryan?"

"Hello. Yes, that's me. I was here last year as a matter of fact... y'know, for an interview. It went quite well."

The disinterested admin assistant didn't even glance up from her paperwork.

"Oh. Good."

"Well, not that good, or I wouldn't be back here again, would I? Ha-ha-ha!"

She waited politely for me to stop laughing at my own quip.

"Out into the corridor, turn left and follow the nurse to the Dean's study, if my memory serves me correctly... Yeah?"

"No. Turn right actually, but don't worry, the nurse will go with you. She's waiting outside."

"Oh."

I went out of the door and looked around for my guide. There she is. Wonder if she rememb...? Oh no, it's a different one from last year.

"Nicholas Ryan?"

"Hello, yes. And your name is..."

"Danielle."

"Hello, Danielle. I was here twelve months ago actually so I'm quite familiar with the system. Off now to meet the Dean of Dental Studies again I s'pose..."

"Yes, that's right. Follow me please."

Oooh. I felt a disquieting tremble in the lower bowel department as we set off. Kept it to myself though.

"Yes, it was three Grade Es they asked for last time. Sadly, I came down in physics and chemistry though."

"Oh."

"Gutted I was, Danielle."

"Oh dear."

"Yeah, so I'm hoping they'll offer me a place again for this coming September… y'know, once I've finally got the exams under my belt. D'you think they will or…?"

"I wouldn't know I'm afraid, Nicholas."

She walked too quickly. It was just exacerbating all my nerves-related digestive problems. Slow down a bit while I'm talking, darling, will you?!

"…After all, I'm exactly the same person I was last year don't you think?"

"Well yes, you would be."

"The same person. Yeah. Anyway the point is that we've been through all this before. Went well. Offered place. End of. It must be a mere formality at this stage – all this interview stuff. They're bound to take me after two successful interviews… aren't they?

"You'd certainly like to think so, Nicholas."

We'd arrived at our destination – I saw the 'Dean of Dental Studies' sign on the door. We stopped in a little alcove just off the main corridor with the hustle and bustle of hospital life going on all around us - stretchers, doctors, walking wounded, nurses, students…

"Oh… you've changed the system since last year then?"

"I wouldn't know, Nicholas. Now if you'd just sit on this chair please and wait for the bell. Once you hear it, go straight in through that door there and the Dean and his colleagues will interview you. Good luck."

"Thank you."

On completion of the briefing, my nurse then disappeared back into the medical melee. Pity really, I'd planned to say goodbye to her properly, with a jaunty "Probably see you in September then."

But no. She'd gone. I was alone in the hot seat – waiting for that bloody bell.

My nervousness was by now palpable, especially down towards the end of the digestive tract. I considered various scenarios in preparation for my interrogation, one of them being a quick visit to the lats. I didn't want to miss the bell though, so instead, I started working on my interview tactics.

What if the Dean recognises me and wants me to expand on last year's themes? What if he doesn't recognise me? Maybe one of the others will. I'll tell him we've met befo… No, I won't. Yes I will. Be confident. Be confident. That's the main thing. Be…

As I was chanting my mantra. It happened!

Ding… ding… ding.

The bell! I sprung to my feet, wrenched open the oak-panelled door and barged in.

Blimey!

There wasn't one face I recognised! The Dean himself was in the middle, but not my Dean – no half-moon specs - on his left was a matron, but not my matron and on his right was some deputy I s'pose. Never seen any of 'em before in my life! They seemed united by an expression of amazement at my intrusion. I looked around for a vacant seat. Nothing. Christ, they'd completely altered the interview procedure since last year.

And who's this?

There was a fourth person in the room! A rude person with his back to me. The inquisitors were at least staring in astonished acknowledgement of my presence, but not him! He didn't move a muscle.

First to speak was the Dean of Dental Studies – I knew that because there was a sign in front of him on the desk.

"Erm… Mister…?"

He glanced down at the interview schedule.

"Ryan?"

Oh, thank God. He *does* recognise me!

"Yes, sir."

"That was the clock."

What? The 'clock'?! How did that happen? The ignorant, rude bastard with his back to me deigned to turn round at this point to bask in my embarrassment. He had a faint smile on his face in anticipation of some intense squirming on my part no doubt. I instantly recognised his features from earlier. He was the penultimate student called for appraisal. I was the last one and he was the very man I'd been advising on successful interview techniques not twenty minutes before!

"The clock, sir!? Oh, I see. The clock… it's three o'clock then, is it?"

"Well, just after, Mr Ryan."

"Er… well, very sorry, sir. I heard the bell and… and the nurse said listen for the er… and I'd like to apologise to your interviewee there er… 'Michael' was it? And erm…"

As I spoke, I was awkwardly retracing my steps backwards towards where I estimated the door to be. It's quite a difficult manoeuvre in an unfamiliar room.

"Sorry. I can't apologise enough… again…"

Eventually I reached the door and was fumbling behind my back for the handle… Got it.

"I'll go and sit back outside until you're ready. Er, see you again… soon… sir."

Uh-oh, that was ill-advised. This was no time for flippancy.

Once safely out of the room, I collapsed back on to the chair. What a cock up! Not only had I sabotaged my chances of a successful interview outcome but I'd taken the previous applicant down with me!

Speaking of Michael, after five or so tense minutes, the door flew open and out he came. He glared briefly at me as I mimed a repentant message back at him.

"So Sorry."

Just then, the bell sounded.

Giiiiiiiiiiiiiiiiiiiiiiiiiiiiiing!

Oh that's it. The real bell. More persistent and business-like than the cosy chime that I previously mistook as my invitation to enter.

Never mind, back on the front foot now. Onwards and upwards. Focus. Be confident. Here we go…

I gently pushed open the door and re-entered the Dean's study with as much dignity as I could muster, but I knew from the Dean's expression that I'd probably blown it. I was leading an elephant back into the room with me of course, so I decided to begin by acknowledging the invisible mammoth.

"I do hope that unfortunate incident with the elephant, sorry, BELL, earlier on, hasn't in any way er… prejudiced my chances of an offer for a place here at…"

"Oh no not at all, Nicholas."

Phew!

"We'll be assessing applications over the next week or so and as long as you go on to achieve the three grade C passes we require…"

I chuckled enthusiastically at his little wisecrack as he continued.

"I think you can be quietly confident of acceptance. No promises, mind."

"Oh that *is* a relief, sir. Good to know."

WHAT?! He's *not* joking! Grade Cs?!!! Where's my Dean with the easy Es?!

Following an awkward and uncomfortable interview, I was eventually discharged.

"Well thank you, Mr Ryan. That's about it. I think we have all we need. We'll be in touch soon."

I opted for one last ingratiation before leading Dumbo quietly out of the Dean's study.

"Thank you for your time and… may I just apologise once again for the confusion with the bell and everything, sir."

"Don't worry, Nicholas. Easily done."

"Yes, sir."

Easily done if you're a hapless idiot!

I scarpered out of Guys and back to the sanctuary of sunny Southend.

Sure enough, a few days later, a letter arrived from Guy's congratulating me on my successful application for a place at the Dental Hospital – provided I attain three Grade Cs.

Three Grade Cs? Out of the question!

I had to read it twice to take it in! So the mean Dean definitely *wasn't* joking!

Watch my lips, Deano! Grade Cs are way beyond my reach... absolutely out of the question! As I've already demonstrated, Grade Es are tough enough to snare – never mind Cs! What are these people playing at? Talk about 'picky'! I mean they won't have *anyone* on their damn dental course at this rate!

Over the next few days my mood sluggishly wavered from outrageous indignation to reluctant acceptance of the inevitable truth.

I slowly came to the conclusion that it was high time to ditch the dental dream.

Yup. It'll be back on the dustbins for me come September. Rochford Rural District Council, here I come.

Can't wait to see the lads again.

If only my interview had been scheduled for *eleven* o'clock, I might never have made that silly mistake. On the other hand...

35

A WORD IN HIS EAR

By the time he was four years old, our eldest son Patrick had been to Greece six times and his younger brother Alex three times. We were in the habit of holidaying in Epirus, Western Greece, twice a year. We first discovered the place as a couple and later on as a family.

We'd found our Shangri-La. An unspoiled village, with a perfect climate, boat excursions, comfortable apartment accommodation and of course our holiday hosts, the Psoli family. The family was identical to our own, comprising four members – the two parents, Helios and his wife Lacta and Tossas and Smiros, their two sons. Our hosts couldn't do enough for us – their generosity knew no bounds.

Patrick had been holidaying with us in Greece since he was nine weeks old and consequently he was quite relaxed in the company of Greek people. Each time we went there he became more and more confident and when we taught him the Greek version of a few everyday phrases like 'Please', 'Thank you' and 'Good morning', he seemed to enjoy trotting out the words on demand.

It never failed to amuse and delight the Psoli family and Patrick soon realised that it was a crowd pleaser. Unfortunately though, his pronunciation was marred by a persistent lisp which turned *'Yassou'* into *'Yathou'* etc. His ear, however, was quite attuned to the sound of the Greek language.

Now for some inexplicable reason, at the start of this particular holiday, Patrick and Smiros took it into their heads to insult each other at every opportunity. Whenever and wherever they met, verbal abuse would be the order of the day.

Sadly, the impact of this 'savage abuse' was somewhat diminished by the fact that both contestants were competing despite severe impediments. Our friend Smiros was Greek with a very limited offensive vocabulary and our son Patrick, at four years old and about twenty years younger than his opponent, had no concept whatsoever as to how a potent insult might be created. This deficiency was compounded, of course, by the aforementioned lisp.

You'd regularly hear the two of them exchanging feeble put-downs – often including a reference to the TV show 'Thunderbirds' which was a popular kids' programme of the time in England.

"Ah hello there my dear friend Patrick, *you are just a Thunderbirds midget! Misfit. Biscuit!*… No, er…"

"Oh, it's you ith it, Thmiroth? *You thilly… tree!*"

"*Kalimera*, Patrick. So we meet again, *you Kentucky Fried Kitchen. Sorry, Chicken!*"

"Yeth and *you are juthta… a… Thunderbirds broom!*"

Patrick would merely dub Smiros something he could see, like a lemon or a car, a stone or lizard. Smiros on the other hand was far too ponderous. He was constantly refreshing the grammar, vocabulary and syntax of his English abuse until everyone around him had lost the will to live (or least the will to holiday).

It could not be denied that this unlikely pair was absolutely incapable of potent character assassination, yet their witless drone permeated the entire fortnight! A couple of times they were even asked to stop, such was the tedium of their awkward exchanges.

"Give us a break, lads!"

That was the phrase I taught the Greek contingent to shout and they'd regularly call for a pause in the verbal jousting using the cockney accent they'd learned. Of course the laughter that ensued would merely encourage the two protagonists to re-commence their dodgy duels.

And so the fortnight ploughed on...

As I explained before, one regular feature of our holidays in Greece was the kindness of our friends and hosts, the Psoli family. They'd always allocate us one of the family's two cars upon our arrival at the apartments and we were also given the use of two motor scooters for shopping and trips around the village.

It's no wonder that we returned to the little town of Parga over and over again.

They'd even pick us up from the port at Igoumenitsa which was about 40 kilometres away!

The logistics of the journey to Epirus at that time included a flight from Gatwick to Corfu, taxi from Corfu airport to the ferryboat terminal, ferry to Igoumenitsa and then the final stage by car from Igoumenitsa to 'Lacta's Apartments'.

Whenever we arrived at Igoumenitsa, there was always a member of the family or their close circle of friends to chauffeur us all the way to our beautiful destination. Our holiday really began at that moment. We were in the company of friends as soon as we stepped off the ferry.

When the time came to leave Parga and head home, it was understood that one of the family or their friends would deliver us back to the ferryboat departure point in good time for the boat to Corfu and the airplane back to Blighty.

The short straw at the end of this particular holiday was drawn by Smiros, who arrived at the apartments in good time for the journey.

There was a small deputation of Greeks too, including Psoli family members, cleaning ladies, olive harvesters and our favourite bouzouki player Alekos, after whom we'd named our second child.

We said tearful goodbyes to one and all and piled into the Psolis' latest acquisition – a shiny, brand new, black Mercedes!

We were off!

"Bye, see you next year!"

The powerful engine revved and with *yassou*-waves from all windows, we sped off to Igoumenitsa.

It will come as no surprise to learn that the usual pissy insults were exchanged between Patrick and Smiros during the early stages of the journey as the family's brand new Mercedes negotiated the country roads. Smiros was at the wheel but he was in no mood for verbal duelling that particular morning since, prior to departure, he'd been informed that our younger son Alex was prone to vomiting during car travel! Smiros' banter was therefore rather half-hearted. He was distracted by the possibly imminent risk that the child would be redecorating the interior of the new Merc in a shade of vivid green.

We did actually pull over at one point, lowered the side window and directed the infant's mouth towards dusty tarmac. Alex projectile-vomited the contents of his stomach onto the Greek road surface (and several 'spatters' onto the Teutonic paint job) but fortunately, there was no staining of upholstery. Soon we were back on the road and racing towards Igoumenitsa.

Patrick initiated a half-hearted insult session after the regurgitation incident but Smiros was having none of it. He was transfixed by the infant lest a second chunder were on the agenda.

As we swerved into the port and the Merc ground to a halt, our chauffeur encouraged an immediate evacuation of the car (presumably based on the 'quitting whilst ahead' principle.) We could see our ferryboat approaching, so we watched as it docked and the incoming vehicles were off-loaded. This was our cue to buy tickets for the cruise over to Corfu and of course, say our goodbyes to dear Smiros.

Last to say goodbye to each other were the two insult specialists, Patrick and Smiros. It seemed entirely appropriate that their salutations would include a withering insult apiece.

A (by now) relieved and relaxed Smiros was the first to engage.

"So... my tiny friend Patrick, I hope you will have a good winter *you Thunderbirds dunderhead!*"

"Well... thank you *my thilly friend Thmiroth you... er...*
He squinted out to sea.
...ferryboat!"

With that, the four of us made our way over to board the ferry while Smiros was scurrying back to the Merc.

As we walked I became suddenly dissatisfied with the unrewarding standard of repartee which had dogged the previous fortnight. I'd had enough of these puny pokes, these juvenile jibes. So I crouched down next to Patrick and whispered in his ear for a few moments. He listened carefully to my suggestion for a fitting farewell.

He then shouted the phrase perfectly – at the top of his little voice.

"*Thmiroth!!*"

The electric window of the Merc slowly slid open.

"What, Patrick?"

"GOODBYE, THMIROTH, *YOU MOTHERFUCKER*!!!!!"

That's my boy!

Your turn, Smiros.

A shocked reply bounced back as the driver's window skimmed shut.

"OK, OK, Patrick. You have the last word!"

Game set and match.

You should have seen Mummy's face!

36

RONALD AND RONALD

Now I make no bones about it, I cannot march. Never bothered with it. Never needed to really… Quite honestly, I've always considered my failure to retain names as a much more debilitating deficiency.

Marching though… it's just not something that ever came into my world. I think as a boy scout I may have paced a few steps but as for serious marching… no.

There's a good bit of coordination involved with credible marching, of course.

My own particular self-taught approach is where the left arm moves in time with the left leg and the right arm with the right leg, instead of the other way round. It makes you look like a prize prat.

So a prat-in-action is what viewers saw on national television at peak time one Saturday evening, when I first unveiled my unique marching style to the general public.

Like the prat that I am, I was ignorant of the fact that my name was languishing way down at the bottom of a list of Equity members available for hire. Ignorant, that is, until I received an unexpected telephone call from a BBC casting executive.

She introduced herself and explained that she was under pressure to book a lot of singer/actor types for a light entertainment comedy show which regularly featured a musical segment towards the end of each programme. Normally the producers needed just five or six singers per episode but apparently coming up soon, was a big musical production involving at least thirty thespians, all playing Canadian Mounties.

The requirement for so many musical participants had led this poor woman on an excursion down to the murky depths of the very nadir of the Spotlight Directory, where the least-talented Equity union members reside.

As luck would have it, my contact details were down there, just waiting to be accessed.

She wasn't in the habit of booking losers like me, she explained, but the numbers had to be made up somehow.

I sympathised with her plight as I reached for my diary. I sensed an imminent entry, prompted by the woman's obvious desperation.

"Would you be available for a rehearsal on Wednesday at 3pm 'til 5 and recording on Saturday 10am 'til 4?"

See? Thought so.

"Oh, most certainly." (The semi-professional and untalented are always available.)

"Perfect. Thank you, Nick. Goodbye."

Wow! I'd soon be on the telly with Eric & Ernie… was it? Who did she say? French & Saunders? Mike & Bernie? Er… the Chuckle Brothers? No. Can't remember. Whoever it was, I was going to be working with them.

So a couple of days later the script for the show's musical medley arrived in the post. Oh no! Music notation. I don't do dots. I'll have to practise and learn all these damn songs!

I called a musician friend of mine - a proper musician, who could read music and everything - and he played 'one finger' piano versions of all the melodies into a cassette recorder for me so I could learn them. They were all parodies of well-known tunes with humorous lyrics substituting for the original words. Flanagan & Allen would sing the new solo bits and we'd... no, hang on, it was er... Hinge &... Bracket I think... wasn't it? Doesn't matter.

It took a bit of doing anyway, learning how the songs segued into each other and changed key. I seemed to be listening to this tiresome collection every minute of every day leading up to the Wednesday, when at 3pm we all assembled in West London for the choreography rehearsals. Choreography? Just a bit of marching, someone explained.

Shouldn't be a problem...

It was complicated enough though. Even Ant & De... or was it Cannon & Ball... had a few initial problems but after a couple of hours' rehearsal, we were discharged and told to regroup on Saturday at a recording studio in Acton. We'd be recording the music in the morning and then adjourning to the BBC Television Centre to perform the songs on camera in the afternoon.

I dutifully arrived at the studio nice 'n early on the Saturday morning and gave my musical crib sheet a last couple of blasts in the car before heading nervously inside to record.

It all went well and then we were dismissed until 2pm.

During the lunch break, I got chatting with a Swingle Singer who was a regular contributor to the Abbot & Costello Sho… or whoever they were, and was consequently recruited from the top end of the Equity list. He regaled me with funny tales of previous sessions.

Apparently, one time they hired a singer who knew nothing at all about the world of light entertainment. His entire experience had been gleaned in operatic circles. He'd performed only in concert halls around Europe and was unfamiliar with both the personalities and the comedic songs that he'd been booked to perform. I presume that even 'Happy Birthday' would have been a stretch for this fella.

When he did open his mouth, a jarring vibrato and ubiquitous clash of musical genres made shit of the parodies, and his mock Italian accent rendered most of the lyrics incomprehensible.

He had to go… especially following his one and only interaction with the stars of the show. Apparently in ignorance of their status and under duress from the director, he foolishly addressed the diminutive one with the words…

"Out of my way, short-arse!"

He was immediately frogmarched from the studio by two stocky security guards and never seen again – much to the relief of Little… or was it Large?

S'pose it was Little.

After lunch, we all made our way to the BBC's costume department where we were transformed into thirty members of the Royal Canadian Mounted Police. We were sporting ill-fitting red jackets, black trousers, black welly boots painted brown and of course the distinctive Stetson hats.

Rehearsals began in earnest. We were now miming to the recording that we had made earlier on, so we didn't have to worry about the singing too much.

Just the marching. Not that I was worried.

Reeves and, er, Mor... yeah, Mortimer I think, had joined us by this stage and the production team was experimenting with camera moves, checking the autocue and lights 'n things.

After the first full run-through, a homosexual of indeterminate status approached me and enquired:

"Excuse me, how're y' legs?"

"Oh... not too bad, thank you."

Nice of him to ask, but honestly I felt fine.

"Have you marched before?"

"No. Hardly at all!" I couldn't resist a proud giggle of disbelief implying, 'I've really taken to it, haven't I?'

"Just do what the man in front does, yeah?"

"Yes I know! Follow the Swingle Singer."

I may not be a highly experienced marcher but I do get the basic concept. This inquisitive spectator, whoever he was, was beginning to get on my nerves. My legs are just fine by the way, thanks very much. It'd take a lot more than a ten-minute route march around a BBC studio to wear my legs out. They may be a bit spindly but they are functional!

With the benefit of hindsight and having now watched the show, I've come to the conclusion that my inquisitor actually had no interest whatsoever in my legs' well-being but an avid interest in my ridiculous marching style. It was making the entire Mountie platoon look farcical, so he'd been sent down from on high to tell me that I looked a prat and that I should correct my marching style to save everyone else from looking like prats too.

Eventually though, the stranger became bored and with just an acknowledging nod and gesticulation towards Mr Swingle Singer, crept back into the darkness from whence he came – to report no doubt, to his master somewhere up amongst the vision mixers and lighting gantries above.

I, of course, was unaware that I was making a name for myself among the production team, as the 'Mr Bean' (or 'Mr Pastry' for you more mature readers, or indeed 'Corporal Jones') of pretend mounted police and was under the mistaken impression that everything was going swimmingly well.

Over and over we rehearsed and filmed the twelve-minute sequence 'til the director and Cheech & Ch... whoever... were happy.

Although oblivious to the impact I'd had on the music sketch, I now look back on my contribution as added value in the comedy stakes.

I should perhaps have been more cognisant of my marching limitations. Others were and, as a result, I was demoted and suddenly relieved of all further marching duties. I was sent off to join the horse-handling team where I remained shovelling shit for the rest of the taping.

Then, within seconds of hearing the cry "It's a wrap!" I was back in the car and hurtling round the M25 to the relative safety of the A127 Southend turn-off! Somehow I was feeling slightly uneasy about my performance.

We move now to a couple of months later, when I was asked to record a parody of the song 'Convoy' for use as a television commercial in Ireland. The song's subject was the CB radio system that truckers use to communicate with each other on the road and it features a bass singer with a strong American accent.

When it came to casting the singer for this job, I was keen to find an authentic North American accent with a deep tone, as it was a prominent feature of the original. I looked at all my casting information and listened to many a showreel, but I just couldn't find the right voice. Until… I suddenly remembered that one of my Mountie compadres on 'The Two Johnnies' was exactly the man I was looking for. His name was Carl and I traced him through the BBC, contacted his agent, and booked him to sing on my 'Convoy' project.

On the day of the recording, I was in the studio working on the female background vocals until Carl was due. I wasn't expecting him to remember me or our connection, but I thought he'd probably recollect the TV show with the Mounties theme.

Before long, a call came through that he'd arrived at the studio and he was ushered into the control room by one of the receptionists. I stepped forward and introduced myself as we shook hands.

"Hello Carl, I'm Nick Ryan. Nice to meet you again."

He looked surprised.

"Hi… Again?"

"Yes, we've worked together once before…"

"Oh."

"A few months ago… the Mountie thing on 'The Two Krankies'. The BBC. You must remember, there were about thirty of us."

"Oh yeah, that's right. I do remember. The Mountie thing… You know some o' those guys down the front, they couldn't even march!"

"Sorry? Couldn't even march? …er…"

I needed time to think. What an awful shock! This man's sole enduring memory of our previous encounter was my inability to march! It was so indelibly etched into his memory that he felt it necessary to recall the awkwardness within seconds of our reintroduction. Could it really have been that bad? Could it?

I still needed time. I was immediately hell-bent on concealing my identity as the non-marcher of the marching Mounties yet, after what seemed quite a long time, the best I could muster was a return to my established theme.

"Couldn't even march?! You're kidding me!"

I accompanied this last comment with a fleeting demonstration, designed to convince any suspicious observer that I was certainly not the rogue marcher. Those three paces I demonstrated across that small studio control room in semi-darkness, was *no* problem. Look, Carl! *Easy!*

I didn't keep it going too long though, 'case I was rumbled. Now what?

Maybe just a touch more incredulity…

"Unbelievable, Carl! Couldn't even do *this? It's* so basic!"

"I know… When Ronnie saw the playback he went berserk! 'What the hell's going on down at the front?' he shouted… *We're* s'posed to be the funny guys round here! Christ!' He even went looking for 'em he was so pissed."

I chose to remain in disbelief mode… and, more importantly, in a shadowy corner of the control room. I gave it all the incredulity I could muster.

"Couldn't march at all you say…"

"Nope. Not one step, my friend. No coordination."

"But it's hardly rocket science is it, Carl? And then Ronnie went out looking for them, you say."

"Yeah, but I think by then they'd left."

"Well, they had! Probably… gone, Carl. Embarrassed! D'you think? Eh? Scuttled off home."

There was no immediate response to my suppositions. Carl was busy squinting into my shadowy corner – scanning my facial features.

"Erm… sure."

The abolition of National Service has a lot to answer for. Don't you think?

37

THE PILGRIMAGE

At this time, nearly twenty years after the turn of the century, one of the hardships of life in rural Ireland is mobile phone coverage. It's patchy, with every kind of technical frustration known to man, from signal drop out, distortion and interference, to reverberant echo and volume drops blighting every conversation.

Even though, according to 2018 research, 97% of Irish consumers have access to either a smartphone or tablet, the service for many customers is… erratic, to say the very least.

Take our own situation for example.

We endure a 'three tier' service. Inside our home there's no practical mobile phone signal whatsoever, outside our home there's a spasmodic service and outside our home but at a very specific location in the garden, there's an almost tolerable service.

Our house is located in a fairly isolated and mountainous area where the topography plays havoc with every aspect of the phone's efficacy. In fact, it's true to say that hunky-dory mobile telephonic communication to and from our house demands one to dress up warmly and vacate the building!

Yes. To send or receive, we have to traipse outside and shout or tap against a potential background of whistling wind, cattle-moos, birdsong, pelting rain, tractors, strimmers and sheep. This is, of course, where our invaluable 'texting togs' come into their own.

It's fine when you're expecting a call – you just get togged up and loiter outside in the general vicinity of 'the live area' until you connect with your caller. You then shout or tap in response to the feeble signal on offer. Conversations are regularly peppered with phrases like;

"Sorry? What? There's an echo on the li… Say that again… No, I'm losing yo… Hello? Can you hear?"

Now. Back to the regalia. Our togs include a stout jacket with mandatory pencil and pad in the inside pocket, wellies and a hooded plastic mac. It may well be a smartphone we're dealing with here but there's nothing smart about the get-up.

The managing of an *un*expected call is considerably more challenging than a pre-arranged conversation, due to the element of surprise involved. At the shrill chiming of an incoming call, our family members suddenly burst into action and are found frantically togging up in the hall, as they struggle to access the 'live area' outside.

Sad to say, we're all too familiar with that dreaded silence, the desolate emptiness and familiar beep that spells 'missed call'.

We shuffle back indoors, willing the mysterious caller to try again.

Nothing.

We reluctantly de-tog.

However… in all fairness to our mobile service provider, I mustn't paint *too* bleak a picture of the mobile phone services here in the Kingdom of Kerry, because when it really, really matters, we can always activate tier three: the 'gold' service.

You see - at an elevated position in our garden, to the right of the house, where mountainous terrain holds no sway over cell phone technology - we've discovered the absolute Rolls Royce of portable phone clarity!

For the more tenacious of mobile phonists – those who simply must make or receive a call 'cos it's really, really, *really* important, or for those in need of emergency assistance, or for those willing to go to the very ends of the earth (well at least the very ends of our field) for a clear, coherent conversation…

We have the answer.

Fair enough, you do have to schlep about thirty five metres from the house, up high above the surrounding pastures and meadows to engage, but believe me it's worth every stumble and fall.

So clear is our connection from around this inhospitable, craggy protrusion, that it's almost a spiritual experience to send and receive with such high fidelity! Such clarity! The words 'Croagh' and 'Patrick' come to mind*.

We even have a special name for this wondrous place with its miraculous support:

'The Rock of Immaculate Reception'.

And right on cue, here's a call coming in!

"Hello? Nick speaking. No, *Nick*, not Mick… Nick! Short for Nicholas. Yes… Oh. OK. No problem. 'Bye."

Blast. Wrong number! Lovely and clear though.

*Croagh Patrick** – The holiest mountain in Ireland. It's located in County Mayo and overlooks Clew Bay. Standing 2,507 feet high, this is a popular destination for bare-footed pilgrims who climb the mountain in meditative prayer, whilst asking themselves why they didn't pack shoes.

IRISH STUFF

38

READY TO ORDER?

We overheard this short exchange 'twixt waitress and customer in the dining room of an exclusive Kerry eatery.

Diner: "And for me, the soup and the chicken please. Oh by the way, are you residential?"

Waitress: "No, I live round the corner!"

39

INTERNATIONAL TERRORIST
AT LARGE

Here is the exact wording of an RTÉ television news item which I saw on the Six One News recently. It was brought to us by a female newscaster who read it out as follows:

"Gardai have today confirmed that they are assisting the Metropolitan police after parcel bombs were sent to London's Heathrow and City airports and also to Waterloo rail station. It's understood that at least one of the packages contained an improvised explosive device. It had an Irish postmark and an Irish return address."

Security services are apparently keen to interview the occupants of 12a, Monahoola Square, Limerick.

40

CALLING ALL ONANISTS

My attention was recently brought to the following paragraphs in publicity material circulated to promote various summer events that were taking place in the West Cork town of Bantry.

'There's a lot to feel good about in Bantry this coming summer, with all kinds of festivals and assorted attractions to enjoy. They include The International Music event, the Literary Festival and even a Barbeque Weekend when cooking skills on the streets will be called upon to feed ravenous locals and visitors alike.

The June bank holiday celebrations kicked things off this year, with everyone donning new boots and socks for the annual Bantry Wanking Festival.'

41

SHOOTING TO KILL

From a local news bulletin on Radio Kerry:

"The gunman made his escape along an alleyway in the centre of the town. He was later apprehended by police near the Royal Canal where he was shot dead several times."

42

AND YOUR TIME STARTS NOW

There used to be on Radio Telefis Eireann, a radio programme which featured the 'Just a Minute Quiz'. It was a straightforward question and answer format against the clock and it involved a contestant on the phone answering quick-fire questions from the programme's host.

Here's one question I remember very well:

"Now, Mary. Which word beginning with the letter C is often found in a swimming pool?"

"Er… Chlamydia?"

Here are some other allegedly genuine responses attributed to the quiz. These answers were widely publicised in the media at the time of the quiz's host, Larry Gogan's (RIP) transfer to RTÉ Gold. I can't vouch for the answers' authenticity, but hopefully they'll induce a smile.

"What was Hitler's first name?"
"Heil."

"Which star do travellers follow?"
"Joe Dolan."

"Where is the Taj Mahal?"
"Er, just opposite the Royal Dental Hospital."

"Name an occupation in which a torch might be used."
"A burglar?"

"Can you divide forty-eight by sixteen?"
"Yes."

"What is the capital of France?"
"F."

"Name something that you open other than a door."
"Your bowels."

"Name something that a blind man might use."
"A sword."

"What musical instrument has forty seven strings?"
"A violin?"

43

CRAFTSMEN RELAXING?

Whilst driving along in my car one day, I switched on the radio and tuned into Radio Kerry (or Kerry Radio as the audience insists on calling our local radio station) to catch the Kingdom's latest news. It was the weekend I remember... a time when relief and part-time newsreaders were often employed to cover for the 'pros'. The rural accent of the newsreader that day quite caught my attention.

The young man was ill at ease communicating with his listeners.

"And the annual social of the... erm... 'Kerry... Teak... er, Window Association' will take place em... on Thursday the fifteenth at the Killarney Heights Hotel.

And now for the, er... the sports news." As I listened, I began to wonder what exactly the 'Teak Window Association' might be and what was its function. I supposed that it was perhaps an organisation set up to promote the benefits, both aesthetic and practical, of teak hardwood window frames as opposed to plastic or aluminium products.

As I was pondering this master-crafter conundrum, our odd-job newsreader made a dramatic return to the live microphone and consequently, Kerry's airwaves. The News outro music abruptly faded and your man blurted out a big beg-pardon to the audience. He was slightly breathless…

"Apologies! We have a slight correction to an earlier news item… the, er… the annual social of the 'Kerry… *Taekwondo* Association' will take place on Thursday the fifteenth at the Killarney Heights Hotel.

Sorry about that.

Next, the, er… the weather."

"Sorry, the sport next. No, sorry, the deaths!"

I wonder if he persevered with a career in broadcasting.

44

FANCIFUL

As you're probably aware, a number of scenes in recent Star Wars films featured Ireland's Skellig Islands which lie thirteen kilometres off the coast of County Kerry.

As you can imagine, the logistics of transporting all the paraphernalia and personnel involved in filmmaking from the mainland over to the islands is a complicated endeavour.

Hence the need for local cooperation.

Teams of drivers, boatmen and extras would be recruited locally and employed for the duration of the shoot.

As 'members of the team', these people were later (some ten months or so) rewarded for their important contributions by receipt of an invitation to a special screening of the finished film! It took place at Killarney Cinema and was attended by many locals from outlying Kerry towns and villages.

Quite an event it was, with some of the actors present, some politicians, a few producers, local radio and national TV presenters, photographers, drivers, caterers, and so on.

I happened to be waiting in the foyer of the cinema as the Star Wars party filed out of the Cineplex having just viewed the zillion dollar creation. My attention was attracted by two oldish men. They shared weathered, ruddy complexions so I took them to be boatmen – farers of the sea, probably responsible for running equipment and people from mainland for the shoot.

Just as they passed in front of me, one of them turned to the other and delivered a succinct, two-word critique of the soon-to-be blockbuster.

"Bit far-fetched eh, Tom?"

Without a word, his companion raised both eyebrows in perfect accord.

Too late now of course, but a few more tractors on screen might've won 'em over.

45

HAVING A *WONDERFUL* TIME

Now this may be a small bit of a generalisation, but it would be fair to say that the people of Ireland are not exactly renowned for their attention to detail (as may be evidenced by this generalisation!).

Consider this example which, in leaflet form, was circulated around the country to promote a local water and activity destination. I'll call it Spa Leisure Park.

The wording of the publicity material listed all the attractions available at Spa with the following words.

'Introducing Spa Leisure Park Kenmare - Fun for all the family!

Try your hand at kayaking, canoeing, boating, orienteering, hiking, mountaineering, water-skiing, river cruising… and *hore*-riding'.

Sounds good.

Always nice to vary up the ol' routines a bit, isn't it?

46

SOMETHING HOMER
MIGHT SAY

A few years ago, it was decided that the Irish telecommunications company Eircom would be given a new image, name and identity which would update the company in consumers' minds.

After several months of deliberation, they came up with 'Eir'. (pronounced 'Air') It was an inspired choice in that it linked with the previous name 'Eircom', but also acknowledged a connection with the Norse Goddess of Healing, implying both reliability and experience.

On the day of the relaunch, the newspapers announced with some panache and trumpeting that the remodelled company was ready for relaunch and had been renamed, not as Eir but as…

Dir!

Funny how that mistakenly substituted and uncorrected consonant always makes me think of the boss of the Simpson household in a frustrated mood.

"Dir!!"

'It'll be grand' was the likely reaction from whoever was responsible for checking the spelling of the new name.

Come on, lads! It's only three little letters!

47

JUST PITCH UP

I once rang a local restaurant in Kerry to book a table for a dinner reservation. My call was answered and dealt with very efficiently.

"Hello, Eugene's Cuisine."

"Oh hello, I wonder if I could book a table for two at your restaurant please – 8 p.m. on Thursday."

"Er… well, no, I'm afraid not. We don't take bookings. It gets a bit messy."

Oh! Not *half* as messy as *not* taking them!

It must be like a tardis in there.

48

ONE WORD ANSWER

"And Nick (in purple suit) did you compare the duplication of readership between the two publications?"

"… Er… no."

"Oh. Right. OK, so you didn't… er…"

"No."

ACKNOWLEDGEMENTS

Thank you to Robin Slater for providing a very personal and touching foreword. It was Robin's idea that Nick should commit some of his many anecdotes and stories to paper, and we're so grateful that he took this advice.

Edited by Patrick Ryan and Sue Ryan. Illustrations by Alex Ryan, completed by Dom Hoskins. The front cover design was a joint effort by Dom and Alex, with Dom putting his graphic design skills to great use. You can see more of his work on domhoskins.com

All proceeds from the sale of this book will be donated to the Kerry Hospice Foundation, which provides vital funding to Palliative Care Services in County Kerry, Ireland.

Also available from troubador.co.uk - 'Pools of Blue', a novel by Sue Ryan.

ABOUT THE AUTHOR

Nick was born in London on the 1st January 1948, to parents Norah and John Ryan. Sister, Judy, arrived in 1951 and three years later the family moved to Leigh-on-Sea in Essex. Sadly Nick's father died in a car crash when Nick was eight and Judy just five. His maternal grandmother, who hailed from Dingle in Ireland, moved in to help Norah. Nick formed a strong bond with his Granny and enjoyed listening to the tales of her beloved homeland. An enduring affinity with Ireland and its people stirred in him at an early age.

Both parents possessed a great sense of humour, which was passed on to Nick and Judy. Nick found humour in anything and everything, and was fond of the odd jape and wind-up, to which many of his friends and colleagues can attest.

Music also soon became a passion for Nick. He was asked to form a folk choir at St Peter's Church, Eastwood, which is still going to this day, some 55 years later. He played in several bands, supporting The New Seekers on their UK tour one year. He was a composer of many songs (anyone remember Naughty, Naughty, Naughty?), trying his luck often at Eurovision. One of his compositions – co-written with Robin Slater – was runner-up in 1977.

Nick joined the world of advertising, firstly as a media buyer and planner about which, by his own admission, he knew very little. His obvious creative and musical talents were soon put to good use however, as he was asked to help out with a new campaign for Wall's Cornetto and came up with Just One Cornetto, voted the UK's most memorable jingle. Nick worked on many other successful campaigns, notably ones for Bird's Eye products. His deep, rich voice was also used on several ads and other audio productions, and he was the voice of Stig of the Dump and of The Slow Norris from the children's eponymous TV programme.

In the year 2000, Nick and his wife Sue moved their family to the wilds of Southern Ireland, settling in the beautiful location of Bonane, close to Kenmare, County Kerry. Nick felt right at home, immediately forging bonds with neighbours and locals alike. He worked for Radio Kerry for a number of years and was also soon putting his talents to good use locally. He formed a one-man band and became in great demand around Kerry and beyond. One of his favourite regular gigs was at Helen's Bar, Kilmackillogue, during the summer months. Many locals would faithfully turn up on a Sunday afternoon to enjoy his wonderful singing, his witty banter and the light-hearted abuse that was frequently thrown their way. He started the Bonane Church folk choir and the Kenmare Barber Shop choir (known as Mary and the Blow-ins). He also directed several Christmas Pantomimes and co-wrote and directed the acclaimed Bonane Women's play – The Parcel from America.

Nick left us all too soon on 20th May 2022. He is greatly missed by his family, his many friends in Ireland and Britain (and France) and his beloved Bonane community.

He is survived by his wife Sue and their two sons; Patrick, a writer/director and Alex, a professional musician.

The Ryan family, Berlin, February 2016